UNIFIED ACTION HANDBOOK SERIES

This *Handbook for Military Support to Governance, Elections, and Media* is Book Three in a set of five handbooks developed to assist the joint force commander design, plan, and execute a whole-of-government approach. Included with the series is an overview J7/J9 Pamphlet, *Executive Summary of the Unified Action Handbook Series*, that describes the handbooks, suggests how they should be used, and identifies the significant interrelationships among them. The following is a short summary of each handbook:

Book One: *Military Participation in the Interagency Management System for Reconstruction and Stabilization*

The handbook outlines joint force roles and responsibilities in the Interagency Management System (IMS) and existing interagency coordination authorities and mechanisms. It aligns with the *USG Planning Framework for Reconstruction, Stabilization, and Conflict Transformation.* It will also align with the *IMS Guide* under development at the Department of States' Office of the Coordinator for Reconstruction and Stabilization.

Book Two: *Military Support to Essential Services and Critical Infrastructure*

This handbook defines services essential to sustain human life during stability operations (water, sanitation, transportation, medical, etc.), the infrastructure needed to deliver such services, and potential joint force responsibilities.

Book Three: *Military Support to Governance, Elections, and Media*

The last comprehensive guide to military governance was written in 1943. Combatant commanders have directed joint forces to rebuild media, support election preparations, and provide advisors to embryonic executive ministries and legislative committees in recent and current operations. This handbook provides pre-doctrinal guidance for joint force support to good governance, political competition, and support to media.

Book Four: *Military Support to Economic Stabilization*

This handbook outlines joint force support to economic development. It addresses conducting a comprehensive economic assessment, employment and business generation, trade, agriculture, financial sector development and regulation, and legal transformation.

Book Five: *Military Support to Rule of Law and Security Sector Reform*

This handbook defines the "Rule of Law;" explains the interrelationship between rule of law, governance, and security; and provides a template to analyze the rule of law foundation essential to successful stability operations.

NOTICE TO USERS

All approved and current Joint Warfighting Center (JWFC) Pamphlets, Handbooks, and White Papers are posted on the Joint Doctrine, Education, and Training Electronic Information System (JDEIS) Web page at https://jdeis.js.mil/jdeis/jel/template.jsp?title=jwfcpam&filename =jwfc_pam.htm. If a JWFC product is not posted there; it is either in development or rescinded.

PREFACE

1. Scope

This *Handbook for Military Support to Governance, Elections, and Media* provides fundamental guidance, planning considerations, techniques, procedures, and other information for the restoration of a country's governance, elections, and media institutions and processes during the post-conflict[1] period (e.g., post-civil war; Phase IV, "Stabilize," of a major operation).

2. Purpose

This handbook is not intended to stand alone as a planning guide, but instead to complement the planning that would be required to better integrate all elements of national capacity in response to an overseas contingency or in support of military engagement, security cooperation, and deterrence activities. **Its primary purpose is to aid US joint military planners on a joint force staff to more fully understand their roles and tasks in building or restoring a failed government in the immediate post-conflict period.** It is designed to help lay the groundwork for a successful transition between military and civilian authorities in situations where the armed forces for whatever reason find themselves as the *de facto* governing authority responsible for providing or establishing governance.

3. Content

a. This handbook describes the nature of situations that will be faced and provides both general guidance on addressing governance problems and contact references to obtain specialized assistance. It stresses that civilians are generally the supported entity for governance-related operations. It does not address the military roles in longer-term democracy and governance development in state-building missions. It also does not detail military support to security sector reform (SSR) or security force assistance (SFA), although both SSR and SFA have important institution-building and governance components. Joint force support to SSR is substantially discussed in the *Handbook for Military Support to Rule of Law and Security Sector Reform.*

b. The major civilian United States Government (USG), intergovernmental organizations (IGOs), and nongovernmental organizations (NGOs) that play key roles as donors and implementing partners are discussed in the handbook. Understanding the complexity of the "state reconstruction" environment will assist planners in achieving a more unified effort with major stakeholders. This handbook also includes assessment and evaluation tools, lists of crucial planning considerations, military tasks matrices, and principles of practice. Vignettes and case studies, informed from on-the-ground experiences, illustrate key concepts and best practices. A special topics section discusses the strategic relationships between governance operations and counterinsurgency, political reconciliation, SFA, SSR, and ungoverned areas.

c. This handbook does not address specific military tasks in the rare cases where a transitional military authority assumes governing responsibilities. Joint publication (JP)

3-57, *Civil Military Operations,* and Army field manual (FM) 3-07, *Stability Operations,* stand as the authoritative references for military governance.[2] Although no longer officially Service doctrine, FM 25-5, the 1943 Army-Navy manual, *Military Government and Civil Affairs,* provides proven methods to conduct transitional military authority.[3]

d. While this handbook defines and discusses potential military roles related to governance, it does not suggest that US forces will always undertake any or all of these activities in any given operation. Furthermore, the handbook does not advocate military governance but simply seeks to identify the governance-support roles and tasks that military forces have performed in numerous missions. With a more robust task inventory, the planner can anticipate and plan for the full range of possible tasks and the concomitant capabilities required in the post-conflict period.

4. Development

a. JP 1-02, *Department of Defense Dictionary for Military and Associated Terms,* defines unified action as, "The synchronization, coordination, and/or integration of the activities of governmental and nongovernmental entities with military operations to achieve unity of effort." To this end, United States Joint Forces Command (USJFCOM) embarked on a multi-year "Unified Action" project to carry forward the principles of unified action through concept development and experimentation. This project focused on two lines of operations (LOOs) to achieve its objectives. The first line included limited objective experiments contributing to the implementation of the DOD work plan to support National Security Presidential Directive 44 (NSPD-44). The second LOO included spiral events to produce a series of handbooks and overview (see inside of the front cover). The products of both LOOs were developed and validated through a rigorous process of experimentation that was conducted with military and civilian partners across the United States Government.

b. This handbook was developed in close coordination with, and used significant input from, both civilian and military subject matter experts. The authors also regularly vetted the content with these experts to assure currency and accuracy of both theory and practice. As a result, it represent the current state of best practices in the development and restoration a country's governance.

c. An important issue which arose during the drafting of this handbook is the widespread use of jargon and acronyms that may not translate particularly well between various agencies within the US Government. Insofar as possible, the authors have attempted to improve the readability of this handbook by using common terms in plain English. This handbook also includes a glossary of terms commonly used within the interagency community that may not be familiar to military planners.

5. Application

This handbook is not approved joint doctrine, but is a non-authoritative supplement to current stability operations doctrine that can assist commanders and their staffs in planning, executing, and assessing governance, elections, and media development and restoration activities. The information herein also can help the joint community develop stability operations doctrine, mature governance concepts for possible transition into joint doctrine, and further the effectiveness of military support to governance restoration in joint operations. This handbook should be treated as a guide and not as a template. It is important to understand the dynamic nature of interagency coordination and not it as step-by-step "how-to" manual. **Commanders should consider the potential benefits and risks of using this information in actual operations**.

6. Distribution and Contact Information

a. Distribution of this handbook to US Government Agencies and their contractors is authorized. Other requests for this document shall be submitted to USJFCOM, Joint Concept Development and Experimentation, Attn: Maj Arnold Baldoza, 115 Lake View Parkway, Suffolk, VA 23435-2697; or by phone to Maj Arnold Baldoza at 757-203-3698.

b. Comments and suggestions on this important topic are welcomed. The USJFCOM JWFC points of contact are Lt Col Jeffrey Martin, 757-203-6871, jeffrey.martin@jfcom.mil; and Mr. Mike Lawrence, 757-203-6716, michael.lawrence.ctr@jfcom.mil

DAN W. DAVENPORT
Rear Admiral, U.S. Navy
Director, Joint Concept Development
& Experimentation, J9

STEPHEN R. LAYFIELD
Major General, U.S. Army
Director, J7/Joint Warfighting Center

Intentionally Blank

TABLE OF CONTENTS

PAGE

CHAPTER I
INTRODUCTION AND OVERVIEW

* Background and Intent I-1
* The Military Problem I-1
* Current Military Guidance on Governance-Support I-2
* Military History in Supporting Governance I-3
* The International Framework for Military Support I-4
* Governance Defined I-6
* Other Relevant Definitions I-8
* Principles of Best Practice I-10
* Key Partners in Governance Strengthening and Support I-12
* Key Partners and Unified Action I-15

CHAPTER II
MILITARY SUPPORT TO POST-CONFLICT GOVERNANCE

* Introduction II-1
* Strategic, Policy and Program End States II-2
* Conflict and Governance Assessments II-3
* USAID's Post-Conflict Assessment Process II-4
* Coordination of Assessments II-7
* Assessment and Gender II-9
* USAID Planning II-10
* Military Tasks and Planning Considerations for Post-Conflict
  Governance and Participation II-10
* Constitutional Processes II-11
* Interim and Transitional National Governance II-14
* Interim and Transitional Local Governance II-19
* Creating or Strengthening Viable Legislative Processes II-25
* Political Parties II-29
* Civil Society II-35
* Special Governance Topics II-38
* Security Force Assistance, Security Sector Reform, and Governance II-45
* Ungoverned Areas and Safe Havens II-49
* Governance and Counterinsurgency II-51
* Summary of Military Tasks and Planning Considerations II-53

CHAPTER III
MILITARY SUPPORT TO POST-CONFLICT ELECTIONS

* Introduction and Military Problem III-1
* Strategic Election Planning, Programming, and Budgeting III-2

- Operational Planning for Elections III-7
- Military Tasks in Post-Conflict Elections III-10
- Planning Considerations III-17
- Key Agencies and Implementing Partners III-20

CHAPTER IV
MILITARY SUPPORT TO MEDIA DEVELOPMENT AND INFORMATION
   DISSEMINATION

- Overview IV-1
- The Military Challenge IV-1
- Media Assessment IV-2
- Media Development IV-4

APPENDICES

A   Military Tasks for Support to Post-Conflict Governance A-1
B   Principles and Tasks for Military Support to Post-Conflict Elections B-1
C   Comparing Assessment Frameworks C-1
D   References and Web Sites for Key Stakeholders, Donors, and Implementing
     Partners D-1
E   Endnotes E-1

GLOSSARY

Part I   Abbreviations and Acronyms GL-1
Part II Terms and Definitions GL-4

FIGURES

II-1   Assessment Process II-5

TABLES

II-1   Foreign Assistance Planning/Programming Documentation at the
       USAID Mission Level II-12
IV-1 Building Media Tasks IV-9
A-1   Military Tasks for Support to Post-Conflict Governance A-1
B-1   Elections Operations Support B-1
C-1   Comparing Assessment Frameworks C-1

CHAPTER I
INTRODUCTION AND OVERVIEW

"In the long-term effort against terrorist networks and other extremists, we know that direct military force will continue to have a role. But we also understand that over the long term, we cannot kill or capture our way to victory. Where possible, kinetic operations should be subordinate to measures to promote better governance, economic programs to spur development, and efforts to address the grievances among the discontented from which the terrorists recruit."

Secretary of Defense Robert M. Gates
National Defense University, September 29, 2008

1. Background and Intent

a. The years since 9/11 have witnessed an emerging joint, Service and interagency consensus about the critical role of governance in transforming conflict, promoting national unity, and addressing extremism. Building government, electoral, and media institutions are essential objectives of any post-conflict reconstruction and stabilization mission. Their importance has been noted in the recent development of Service and joint publications on counterinsurgency, counterterrorism, and stability operations. However, there is scant specific guidance available to assist joint force commanders (JFCs) and staffs in developing plans and operations to raise and grow those institutions.

b. Since World War II, the US military has provided considerable support to state-building missions in Japan, Germany, Vietnam, Lebanon, Panama, Croatia, Bosnia-Herzegovina, Kosovo, Haiti, Afghanistan, and Iraq. US military forces have rebuilt radio and television stations, published interim newspapers to communicate with citizens coming out of conflict, provided substantial support for the conduct of elections, and supplied advisors to embryonic key ministries and legislative committees. But the US military's substantial past and present support to governance development is not captured fully in doctrine and or defined in mission tasks lists. The intent of this handbook is to help correct these deficiencies.

2. The Military Problem

a. While post-conflict responses may follow major interventions,[4] civil wars,[5] or "forced regime changes,"[6] one fact is certain: whatever the conflict's genesis, a government will have to be established. Since the absence or failure of governance often precipitates conflict, the presence of a stable, effective government is critical to post-conflict stabilization and recovery.

THE MILITARY PROBLEM

In complex post-conflict environments, how does the joint force commander plan, coordinate and execute operations that will support the establishment or re-establishment of government and a political processes?

- What military tasks are necessary to provide for "first response governing" in post-major combat theaters?

- What tasks and activities can the joint force perform that support the development of national and local government, political, and civil society institutions and processes?

- What are the essential and supporting military tasks for the safe and successful conduct of elections when the Host Nation capacity is damaged or absent?

- How can the military support capacity development of Host Nation security for future elections?

- How can the joint force support the establishment of an independent and objective media?

---

b. The main task for the JFC is to create an environment conducive to the (re)establishment of stable governance. However, **in the post-conflict period, the military's governance-support roles and tasks will extend well beyond the provision of a stable environment**. This is the "Golden Hour" when host nation (HN), donor, development and assistance agencies are absent, scarce, under-resourced or over-burdened. Eventually a myriad of HN and international stakeholders will assume the preponderance of responsibilities in rebuilding the governing, civic and political institutions. **But it is in the period immediately following combat operations that joint forces generally need to take on a broad array of governing and governance-support tasks – likely the most expansive military support to governance than at any other time.**

MILITARY CONTRIBUTIONS TO POST-CONFLICT GOVERNANCE FALL PRIMARILY IN FOUR AREAS

- "First-response" governing when no government exists
- Support to an interim, transitional, or new government
- Elections support
- Building media infrastructure and fostering objective and open media sources.

---

3. Current Military Guidance on Governance-Support

a. State-building and governance support are enjoying a renewed focus in several recent military and civilian publications. The US military role in governance has been most recently set forth in US Army field manual (FM) 3-07, *Stability Operations*.[7] "Support to Governance" is one of five stability tasks identified in FM 3-07. Joint Publication 3-

---

07.3, *Peace Operations*, defines "governance and participation" as one of the mission sectors of a peace building operation. The Joint Staff will soon publish JP 3-07, *Stability Operations*, after combatant command, Service, and Department of Defense agency review. In FM 3-24, *Counterinsurgency*, "governance" is included as a logical line of operation (LOO).[8] These sectors, tasks, and LOOs correspond to the "Governance and Participation" sector identified in the Department of State's Essential Task Matrix (ETM) and to USAID's Democracy & Governance (DG) programs.

b. The importance of strengthening weak, failing, fragile, national and local governments has also been cited in recent Quadrennial Defense Reviews, National Security and Defense strategies, and Department of Defense (DOD) Directives. DOD Directive (DODD) 3000.05 emphasizes that stability operations are no longer secondary to combat operations and goes on to stress that stability operations are likely more important to military success than traditional combat operations. The Directive also acknowledges the pivotal central role of restoring government structures in stability operations.

"NORMAL" OPERATIONS – STABILITY GOVERNANCE

Over its history, the United States has fought only eleven conventional wars. The majority of the hundreds of other military operations carried out are considered stability operations, many of which have a strong governance component. *"Contrary to popular belief, the military history of the United States is one characterized by stability operations, interrupted by distinct episodes of major combat."*[9]

---

4. Military History in Supporting Governance

a. The United States military has a long history of close involvement with governance, and not only in stability operations. In fact, governance by US forces, normally the US Army and US Marines, has usually followed the end of combat operations. During the Mexican War (1846-1848), the US Army established governance programs when it occupied central Mexico. The Spanish-American War (1898) resulted in US military governments in Cuba and the Philippines. The occupations of Japan and Germany at the end of World War II are perhaps the best-known examples of military governance.

MILITARY GOVERNANCE IN THE PHILIPPINES

Following the defeat of the Spanish in 1898, the United States established a military government in Spain's former colony of the Philippines. A succession of three American generals served as military governors until 1901, when civilian government was inaugurated. Under the military government, schools modeled on the US system were introduced, initially with American soldiers serving as teachers. The military government also organized a court system, established local governments and conducted the first local election in 1899.

---

b. During the Cold War, the US military supported governance operations in a wide range of locations, including the Dominican Republic (1965), Grenada (1986), and Panama (1989). The Vietnam War brought the US military into counterinsurgency operations and the formation of CORDS (Civil Operation and Revolutionary Development Support) within the Military Advisory Command. CORDS integrated the military with the United States Agency for International Development (USAID) and the Department of State to implement governance programs directed at gaining the allegiance of the rural population for the Government of Vietnam. The list of examples of military involvement with governance is long and growing.[10]

c. The military role has shifted away from direct military government, as in post-World War II Japan and Germany, to playing a supporting role in governance, often in cooperation with multilateral partners and intergovernmental organizations (IGOs), e.g., the United Nations (UN). Several changes in the characteristics of the post-Cold War international system have altered the military's methods for establishing new governments:

(1) The end of a bipolar world resulted in a much more complex international system, with considerable instability and the emergence of new threats.

(2) The UN became increasingly involved in peace operations, especially with the post-Cold War effectiveness of the Security Council.

(3) The number of stakeholders and interested parties, including nongovernmental organizations (NGOs), has dramatically increased, as has media and public attention devoted to international crises and issues.

(4) The resources of US civilian agencies, USAID, DoS, the Central Intelligence Agency (CIA) and others, never able to match US military resources, declined further with the end of the Cold War.

5. The International Framework for Military Support

a. Since the end of the Cold War, all of the United States' international interventions have included objectives to establish stable governments with legitimate systems of political representation at the national, regional, and local levels. In a stable government, the people regularly elect a representative legislature according to established rules and in a manner generally recognized as free and fair. Legislatures must be designed consistently with a legal framework and legitimate constitution.

b. A USG mission to support the reestablishment of a government and its political and peace processes usually evolves from some form of peace agreement establishing the arrangements and mechanisms under which a country will be governed in the future. The authority for military support for governance usually flows from these agreements, reinforced by UN Security Council resolutions. The context for implementation of governance arrangements can take different forms and may involve a variety of international organizations, although the UN often plays a central role. In all such operations, however, the HN and the designated transitional authority will be the key partners.

c. In cases where US national interests dictate a regime change through US military intervention (e.g., Afghanistan, Iraq), extensive negotiations with key allies and HN representatives will be required to create an international agreement specifying the formation a new government. The US military may play an essential and crucial role in the implementation of these agreements (e.g., Afghanistan).

AFGHANISTAN – THE BONN AGREEMENT

Officially the Agreement on Provisional Arrangements in Afghanistan Pending the Re-Establishment of Permanent Government Institutions - the Bonn Agreement - re-created the State of Afghanistan following the US invasion in response to the September 11, 2001 terrorist attacks. The 2001 Bonn Conference, overseen by Lakhdar Brahimi, UN Special Representative of the Secretary-General for Afghanistan (SRSG), convened prominent Afghans to agree on a plan for governing the country.

The Agreement determined the composition and functions of the Interim Authority, defined the legal framework and judicial system, authorized the deployment of the International Security Assistance Force (ISAF), authorized the role of the UN and the SRSG, and called for "free and fair elections" to be held no later than two years after the convening the Emergency Loya Jirga. Significantly, the Taliban was not present at the negotiations. Some counterinsurgency experts think that the Taliban's absence sowed the seeds for the later insurgency.

---

d. A more common type of agreement that would provide international authority for military support to governance brings together warring factions within a country (e.g., Bosnia-Herzegovina or Cambodia). In these scenarios, belligerents negotiate a peace agreement, brokered by a third nation or group of nations, a regional grouping, or the United Nations. Such agreements usually contain a provision calling for "free and fair" elections to form a post-conflict government and may specify the organization agreed upon by the parties to organize and conduct the election. After the signing of a peace agreement, the UN Security Council usually passes a resolution of support and, if requested, may authorize a peacekeeping force.

THE DAYTON ACCORDS AND MILITARY SUPPORT FOR ELECTIONS IN BOSNIA-HERZEGOVINA

Chapter 1: The NATO-led Implementation Force (IFOR) played a strong role in support of Bosnia-Herzegovina's successful September 14, 1996 elections. The follow-on joint combined force, Stabilization Force (SFOR) also played a substantial and vital role in the 1997 and 1998 elections.

Chapter 3: The authority for IFOR's involvement grew out of The General Framework Agreement (the "Dayton Peace Accords" of November 21, 1995), which formally ended the fighting. In Annex 1A on the deployment of IFOR, the parties agreed that on request IFOR would "help create secure conditions for

---

the conduct by others of other tasks associated with the peace settlement, including free and fair elections." In Annex 3 (elections), the parties also requested the Organization for Security and Cooperation in Europe (OSCE) to plan and supervise "the preparation and conduct of elections." The General Framework Agreement was endorsed by UN Security Council resolution 1031 (15 December 1995).

Chapter 4: In February 1996, the OSCE requested IFOR support with 32 tasks (later reduced to 23) in support of the elections. In addition to providing a secure environment for the elections, IFOR assisted with planning, logistics and communications. IFOR helped in identifying, mapping and checking security at over 4,600 polling stations; in the delivery and subsequent collection of election materials and ballot papers; in the distribution of absentee ballot papers; and in the deployment and transportation of supervisors and observers. On election day, IFOR operated a Joint Emergency Response Center with the OSCE and provided and maintained an extensive communications network. The elections were conducted peacefully with no major disturbances or violence.[11]

6. Governance Defined

*"Ineffective and illegitimate governance usually precipitates conflict and crises. To prevent a return to conflict, efforts must focus on building **effective**, **legitimate** and **resilient** states."*

Organization for Economic Cooperation and Development, "Principles for Good International Engagement in Fragile States and Situations, (April 2007)

a. Governance can be broadly or narrowly defined. There are numerous definitions of "governance" and in some instances terms are used interchangeably with governance, though their meanings are not the identical (e.g., state-building, nation-building, civil administration institution-building, public administration). Some of the most frequently used definitions of governance are:

(1) "…system of values, polices, and institutions by which a society manages its economic, political and social affairs through interactions within and among the state, civil society and private sector. It comprises the mechanisms and processes for citizens and groups to articulate their interests, mediate their differences and exercise their legal rights and obligations. It is the rules, institutions and practices that set limits and provide incentives for individuals, organizations and firms. Governance, including its social, political and economic dimensions, operates at every level of human enterprise, be it the household, village, municipality, nation, region or globe." (UNDP)[12]

(2) "…traditions and institutions by which authority in a country is exercised. This considers the process by which governments are selected, monitored and replaced;

the capacity of the government to effectively formulate and implement sound policies; and the respect of citizens and the state of the institutions that govern economic and social interactions among them." (World Bank)[13]

(3) "...rules, processes, and behaviors by which interests are articulated, resources are managed, and power is exercised in society." (European Commission)[14]

(4) "...process in which a political unit's citizens and decision makers interact to administer the unit, e.g., choose governments, express policy preferences, select policy, enact laws, and create governmental and nongovernmental institutions." (USAID)[15]

(5) " ...state's ability to serve the citizens through the rules, processes, and behavior by which interests are articulated, resources are managed, and power is exercised in a society, including the representative participatory decision-making processes typically guaranteed under inclusive, constitutional authority." (FM 3-07)

b. While some definitions are expansive and others more minimalist, there are common tenets in all: institutions, processes, management of resources, the relationship between state and civil society, leadership selection, and the exercise of power. Governance's multiple dimensions result in programs that vary widely from context to context and between donors. **These many dimensions also explain why (re)establishment of governance in a war-torn and wounded country requires a long-term commitment from the international community.**

DEMOCRATIC GOVERNANCE

State building and good governance do not require a specific form of government, although many argue that key elements of these—legitimacy, accountability, public participation, and responsiveness—are best promoted through democratic government. In simple terms, democracy is government in which the people hold the ruling power.

They do so by electing legislators and the chief executive through regular, competitive, multiparty elections within a framework of political rights, civil liberties, and rule of law. When competitive elections are truly free and fair, they provide a basis for conferring legitimacy on a government. They also provide an instrument for removing underperforming leaders from office, and so provide an incentive for political leaders to govern more effectively. Democracy also gives citizens non-electoral means—associations, movements, the media—to monitor the conduct of public officials and participate in policymaking. Indeed, it is the position of the US government that democracy and good governance together provide the strongest guarantee of security, justice, and economic development.[16]

---

c. While there may be no single definition accepted by all stakeholders, there is a consensus about the goals of a good governance program.[17]

(1) increasing citizen participation and expanding civil society oversight;

(2) strengthening election and political processes;

(3) improving political and administrative institutions and infrastructure;

(4) increasing the capacity of the legal system;

(5) developing responsible media;[18] and

(6) engendering respect for accountable institutions.

7. Other Relevant Definitions

a. In the handbook, **post-conflict** is used to refer to the period following conflict and the cessation of active combat. However, the use of the term in the handbook does not imply that security has been restored, and the post-conflict environment may continue to be hostile or uncertain.

b. **Reconstruction** refers to the process of rebuilding degraded, damaged or destroyed political, socioeconomic, and physical infrastructure of a country or territory to create the foundation for long-term development (FM 3-07). **Stabilization** is defined as the process by which underlying tensions that might lead to resurgence in violence and a breakdown in law and order are managed and reduced, while efforts are made to support preconditions for successful long-term development (FM 3-07). Civilian USG agencies often combine these terms and refer to **reconstruction and stabilization**. In civilian usage, reconstruction and stabilization activities may be conducted by either military or civilian agencies. In hostile or uncertain security environments, these missions may be initially conducted by military forces, but transitioned to civilian agencies when security improves. The area for reconstruction and stabilization operations will frequently be a **failed or fragile state**, a phrase that refers to a country suffering from institutional weaknesses serious enough to threaten the stability of the central government (FM 3-07).

KEY TERMS

"Effectiveness **refers to the capability of the government to work with society to assure the provision of order and public goods and services.**

Legitimacy **refers to the perception by important segments of society that the government is exercising state power in ways that are reasonably fair and in the interests of the nation as a whole. Where both effectiveness and legitimacy are weak, conflict or state failure is likely to result.**"[19]

---

c. Of the several military definitions of **assessment**, the one contained in JP 3-0, *Joint Operations* – the continuous monitoring and evaluation of the current situation and progress of an operation – comes closest to the term's usage by civilian agencies. As used by civilian agencies, assessment refers holistically to the process of consultation, information gathering, and analysis and to the product of that process. In addition, there are many different kinds of governance assessments (pre-election, election commission, election security, parliamentary, ministerial, local government, etc). However, most inventory and analyze the political, social, economic, and security situation in a country or operational area. Similarly, while **evaluation** in joint doctrine (JP 1-02) is an item of information in terms of credibility, reliability, pertinence, and accuracy; civilian aid agencies more typically understand evaluation as the process of determining the progress toward accomplishing a task, creating an effect, or achieving an objective. **Monitoring** is usually partnered with evaluation.

d. In addition to the above terms, the following definitions inform this handbook. These terms do not have corresponding terms in joint doctrine, or they have slightly different meanings for civilian agencies:

(1) **Development** (also international development) encompasses foreign assistance, and includes sectoral issues such as governance, rule of law, human rights, and gender equality. While development is related to foreign assistance, it is distinct from the concepts of security assistance, disaster relief and humanitarian assistance. Development also implies a longer-term perspective and planning cycle.

(2) **Democratization** is the process of political change that moves the political system of any given society towards a system of government that ensures peaceful competitive political participation in an environment that guarantees political and civil liberties. It is sometimes paired with "governance" as in "democracy and governance" or with "political development."

(3) **Public administration** refers to the development and implementation of government policy with the objective of ensuring a well-run, fair, and effective public service. Public administration is carried out by employees (civil servants) who work in government departments and agencies and produce a wide range of government services. This contrasts with **civil administration** in military terminology, which refers to an administration established by a foreign government in (1) friendly territory, under an agreement with the government of the area concerned, to exercise certain authority normally the function of the local government; or (2) hostile territory, occupied by United States forces, where a foreign government exercises executive, legislative, and judicial authority until an indigenous civil government can be established.

(4) **State building or reconstruction** is the effort to build or rebuild the institutions of a weak, post-conflict, or failing state. State building may be undertaken by external governments and organizations, for example following a military intervention or peacekeeping operation. In a post-conflict environment, state building ideally involves external and internal participants constructively engaged in a process that results in political understandings on the form of government, prioritization and initiation of work to restore core government functions, and the provision of government services in response to public expectations. In this context, the term state building is preferable to **"nation building,"** since it focuses on institutions rather than identity (a nation).

(5) **Nation assistance** is civil or military assistance (other than foreign humanitarian assistance) provided to a country by US forces within that country's territory during peacetime, crises, emergencies, or war based on agreements mutually concluded between the United States and that country. Nation assistance supports a HN by promoting sustainable development and growth of responsive institutions. The goal is to promote long-term regional stability. Nation assistance programs often include, but are not limited to, security assistance (SA), foreign internal defense (FID), and Title 10 United States Code (10 USC) programs, such as military civic action (MCA), and activities performed on a reimbursable basis by federal agencies or IGOs. All nation assistance activities are normally coordinated with the US Ambassador through the Embassy Country Team.[20]

8. Principles of Best Practice

a. The following ten "Best Practices"[21] provide a lens for the planner to view all foreign military engagements, interventions and assistance operations. In fact, the joint planner should adapt his or her planning to include these ten as operational design elements[22] and planning benchmarks. They are particularly applicable to the areas of governance support since the goal of such support should be focused on HN sustainability, capacity, capability, and ownership. The end state of governance assistance is always a stable, effective, legitimate, and functioning government.

(1) **Exercise unified action**. Stabilization and reconstruction operations should be planned through a whole-of-government process that builds on a shared situation assessment to define an overarching strategic goal. Once the goal is defined and approved, policymakers must approve a viable strategy to achieve the goal as well as a more detailed implementation plan, integrate them with the HN goals and plans to the degree possible, and collaborate with IGOs and NGOs to achieve coherency.

(2) **Take ownership**. The people of the HN must own the stabilization and reconstruction process and be its prime movers. This can be challenging if the country in question had been invaded or occupied. Engaging the HN government (if one exists) and local government and civil society leaders as early as possible in planning and implementing the recovery process is essential. Strategies to involve local public and private sector entities need to be developed consonant with requirement for risk management and accountability.

(3) **Build HN capacity**. From the earliest stage, an intervention must emphasize (re)building capacity – public and private, national and local. This includes not only state institutions' capacity, but also the capacity for checks and balances on executive power involving the legislature, judiciary, civil society, the private sector and the media. Capacity building requires long-term engagement. Major participants must make an overall commitment to stay engaged over an extended period, otherwise stability may be threatened by spoilers and insurgents who have waited out the initial attention.

(4) **Recognize the Political-Security-Social Nexus**. The political, security, and social development spheres are interdependent: failure in one risks failure the others; donors must therefore balance progress between the sectors.

(5) **Take the Long View, but Show Results Quickly**. Experience demonstrates that without short-term, viable results to show from an intervention, a stabilization and reconstruction environment is likely to continue to deteriorate. Short-term measures are required to meet the needs of the populace and promote a secure environment. In the initial period of operations, this window of opportunity is referred to as the "Golden Hour." However, the urgent need for quick, visible, high-impact measures should be carried out in ways that support longer-term efforts to advance stability, reform, and institutional capacity.

(6) **Learn and adapt**. While integrated planning and operations should begin with a shared assessment of the drivers and dynamics of conflict, the planning process must also include a way to measure progress and evaluate outcome of international efforts. To capture rapidly changing conditions, monitoring and evaluation ("periodic reassessment") needs to include quantitative and qualitative information as well as polling data to assess perceptions.

(7) **Move from reaction to prevention**. Immediate action can reduce the risk of a return to conflict or other crises and contribute to long-term development and security. A shift from reaction to prevention should include sharing risk analyses, acting rapidly where risk is high, looking beyond quick-fix solutions to address root causes of conflict and state fragility, strengthening capacity of regional organizations to prevent and resolve conflicts, and helping fragile states themselves to establish resilient institutions that can withstand political and economic pressures.

(8) **Mix and sequence resources to fit the context**. Unstable states require a mix of programs and policies involving foreign assistance, policy dialogue, military assistance or use of force, economic and financial programs and negotiations, and strategic communication. The role that each should play depends on the nature of the conflict and the phase of the intervention. For example, the first stage of intervention is typically stabilization, which requires immediate action to enforce order, feed the populace, restart basic services, initiate a political transition process, and generate local employment, among others. This may be followed by a second stage in which the conflict's root causes – such as corruption, collapsed economic systems, and political exclusion – are addressed. Additional stages follow to continue to long-term institution building of the government and economy.

(9) **Match goals and resources**. A major cause of mission failure is lofty goals, too many priorities, and insufficient resources to achieve them. The scope of post-conflict operations can be so broad that costs escalate far beyond initial expectations, eroding political will among donor nations and leading to disillusionment in the recipient country. The USG should develop rough orders of magnitude of resource needs for each strategic option proposed to policymakers so they can weigh the risks and tradeoffs. During subsequent planning and implementation, changes to the resource picture should prompt reevaluation of the achievability of the goal.

(10) **Focus on addressing the sources of conflict and instability**. To the extent possible, programming in stabilization and reconstruction environments should focus directly on diminishing the drivers of conflict and instability (rather than just the

symptoms) while building local institutional capacity to effectively address conflict and instability. In post-conflict situations there is often a one-time opportunity to reshape structures to address conflict drivers, improve governance, promote equity, and hasten growth and recovery. Approaches might include the development of structures to include marginalized groups, consensus-building mechanisms, checks and balances, decentralization, transparency measures, and transformation of economic structures.

b. **Governance Support Trade-off**. In addition to the ten "Best Practices," commanders and planners should be aware that there is an ever-present tradeoff in stabilization and reconstruction operations between meeting immediate demands for government services and fulfilling the long-term need to build government capacity. Government services are usually urgently needed to stabilize a fragile domestic political situation and deal with humanitarian crises. However, if generating services rapidly becomes the priority, it risks the possibility that capacity-building activities are neglected, or that bad practices become institutionalized early in the reform process. Using contractors rather than indigenous government resources to meet urgent needs carries the additional risk of undercutting the government's legitimacy in the eyes of the populace.

9. Key Partners in Governance Strengthening and Support

a. Key US Government Stakeholders

(1) The **Department of State (DOS)** has overall policy lead for the USG's state building, governance strengthening, and election support efforts. Within the DOS, the **Bureau of Democracy, Human Rights and Labor** promotes democracy, the protection of human rights, respect for international religious freedom, and worker rights globally. The **Office of the Coordinator for Reconstruction and Stabilization** (S/CRS) is mandated to coordinate USG efforts in reconstruction and stabilization. The office is responsible for leading, coordinating and institutionalizing USG civilian capacity to prevent or prepare for post-conflict situations and to help stabilize and reconstruct societies in transition from conflict or civil strife.

(2) The American Embassy (AMEMB) is one of the primary conduits for planning and coordination. The **Country Team** will generally have at least one political officer, a **USAID** field mission director, and a public diplomacy officer. These officials will be best positioned to advise the JFC on the current situation as well as on programs already sponsored by the host government, the USG, and other bilateral and international donors.

(3) The **US Agency for International Development (USAID)** is the lead implementing agency for post-conflict development assistance. USAID's mission is carried out through four regional bureaus: Africa, Asia and the Near East, Latin America and the Caribbean, and Europe and Eurasia. These are supported by three technical (or pillar) bureaus that provide expertise in democracy promotion, accountable governance, disaster relief, conflict prevention, economic growth, agricultural productivity, environmental protection, education reform, and global health.

(a) The **Office of Democracy and Governance (DG)** is USAID's focal point for democracy and governance programming. The DG office's role is to provide USAID and other development practitioners with the intellectual and technical expertise needed to support democratic development. It provides this expertise for rule of law, elections and political processes, civil society, and governance programs. USAID's offices operate through contracts to implementing partners/NGOs as well as by providing direct grants. In addition, USAID community stabilization programs (CSPs) have historically involved governance.

(b) Other key USAID contacts are the **Office of Military Affairs (OMA)** and the **Office of Transition Initiatives (OTI).** The latter works in post-conflict situations and fragile states using quick impact projects lasting 2-3 years. An OTI representative may be the first USAID contact that military forces make and in the past, OTI has embedded representatives into civil affairs and special forces units.

(c) USAID operating units located overseas are known as **field missions**. USAID field missions are much smaller than a military unit and the planner and operator must appreciate the consequences of those smaller numbers for program planning and execution. Full field missions usually consist of 9-15 direct-hire US employees along with a varying number of other personnel and manage a program of four or more strategic objectives. Medium-sized missions (5-8 US employees) manage a program targeting two to three strategic objectives, and small missions (3-4 US employees) manage programs with one or two strategic objectives. Field missions assist HNs based on an integrated strategy that includes clearly defined program goals and performance targets. **Regional support missions**, also known as regional hubs, host a team of legal advisors, contracting and project design officers, and financial services managers to support small and medium-sized missions. In countries without integrated strategies, but where aid is necessary, regional missions work with NGOs to implement programs that help facilitate the emergence of civil society, alleviate repression, and head off conflict among others.

b. **International Organizations Promoting Democracy and Governance**

(1) The **World Bank Group** provides financial and technical assistance to developing countries around the world. Not a bank in the common sense, this group consists of two development institutions owned by 185 member countries, the International Bank for Reconstruction and Development (IBRD), and the International Development Association (IDA). In addition to funding development efforts, the World Bank provides analysis, advice, and information to member country governments. In the areas related to governance, the World Bank staff offer advice and help to governments in the preparation of draft legislation, institutional development plans, country-level strategies, and implementation action plans and can assist governments in introducing new policies or programs. Of particular interest to US military planners, the World Bank publishes the annual *Worldwide Governance Indicators*, one of the most comprehensive cross-country sets of governance and anticorruption indicators currently available.

(2) Multiple **United Nations** departments and organizations also support governance programs, including:

(a) The **United Nations Development Program (UNDP)** is the UN's global development network of over 166 offices and global partnerships with democratic governance institutions. In the governance area, the UNDP provides core services to support national processes of democratic transitions that focus on:

1. providing policy advice and technical support;

2. strengthening capacity of institutions and individuals;

3. advocacy, communications, and public information;

4. promoting and brokering dialogue; and

5. knowledge networking and sharing of good practices. It is usually the entity that coordinates the work of other UN development organizations on the ground when conditions have stabilized.

(b) The **UN Department of Political Affairs (UN/DPA)** is the focal point for post-conflict peace building in the UN system. The department provides political input in pre-negotiations of peace accords.

(c) The **UN Department of Peacekeeping Operations (UN/DPKO)** manages overall UN peacekeeping operations. At the end of 2007, the DPKO oversaw almost 107,000 military, police, and civilian personnel in 17 peacekeeping missions and three political missions around the world.[23]

(d) The **United Nations Educational, Scientific and Cultural Organization (UNESCO)**. UNESCO's **Communication and Information (CI) Sector** operates programs to promote the free flow of ideas by word and image through its staff at UNESCO Headquarters in Paris and representatives in 27 UNESCO field offices. The CI Sector consists of the **Communication Development Division**, the **Division for Freedom of Expression, Democracy and Peace**, and the **Information Society Division**. UNESCO may fund programs in media development so the planner and commander will want to know if they have a presence in country.

(3) Coordination with the UN begins at the national level with the DOS through the US Representative to the UN. An assistant from one of the Services coordinates primarily with the UN's Office for the Coordination of Humanitarian Affairs (UNOCHA) and Department of Peacekeeping Operations (UNDPKO).[24] The UN organizational structure consists of the headquarters and the operational field elements.

c. **Other Significant Donors and Partners**

(1) The United Kingdom (UK) **Department for International Development (DFID)** helps improve the capability of state institutions and strengthen delivery of

government services in partner countries. In particular, DFID has worked with a number of developing countries to strengthen public financial management systems, helping ensure that money is spent for its intended purposes.

(2) The UK **Stabilization Unit** is an interdepartmental body intended to improve the government's ability to support countries emerging from violent conflict.

KEY POINTS OF CONTACT FOR THE MILITARY PLANNER

Although there is a wide array of organizations with governance assistance mandates and responsibilities, a smaller group is usually present in most post-conflict environments. The dominant donor and international organizations that assess, plan, fund, implement, and evaluate the full suite of governance-support programs – and arrive as soon as possible after major combat has ended – are USAID, UNDP, UN, DFID, and WB.[25] Each will have some kind of plan to restart, support, and strengthen political processes and governance. They should be the military planer's primary points of contact when planning for military support to governance, elections and media development.

---

10. Key Partners and Unified Action

a. In the chaos of the post-conflict period; sharing information, cooperating, coordinating, and collaborating with civilian USG, intergovernmental, international, nongovernmental and HN organizations is one of the earliest and most important challenges facing military forces. The lack of interagency coordination and civil-military cooperation has consistently been identified as a primary shortcoming in US overseas missions. With rising global responsibilities and declining resources, it is critical for all stakeholders – both military and civilian - to combine efforts to maximize assets and capabilities toward creating stable governance and lasting peace. Activities and concepts such as coordination, collaboration, synchronization, harmonization, integration, whole-of-government and comprehensive approaches, and unified action have advanced from the "interesting idea" category to the "absolutely necessary" for the success of stabilization and reconstruction missions.

b. A **whole-of-government**[26] approach relies on interagency coordination among USG agencies. A successful whole-of-government approach depends upon the ability of civilians and military forces to plan, assess, and execute in an integrated, interagency manner. Accomplishing this approach requires a willingness and ability to share resources among USG agencies and organizations while working toward a common goal. Success also requires early and high-level participation of national and multinational civilian and military participants.

A Successful Whole-of-Government Approach Requires that All Stakeholders:

• Are represented, integrated, and actively involved in the process;
• Share an understanding of the situation and problem to be resolved;
• Strive for unity of effort toward achieving a common goal;
• Integrate and synchronize capabilities and activities; and
• Collectively determine the resources, capabilities, and activities necessary to achieve their goal.[27]

---

c. A **comprehensive approach** is an approach that integrates the efforts of the USG's departments and agencies, IGOs and other international organizations, NGOs, multinational partners, and private sector entities to achieve unity.[28] The term "comprehensive approach" entails a broader, more inclusive range of possible organizations and agencies in a reconstruction and stabilization mission with an emphasis on multilateral and international.

d. **Unified action** is the synchronization, coordination and integration of the activities of governmental and nongovernmental entities with **military operations** to achieve unity of effort.[29] Unity of effort is coordination and cooperation toward common objectives, even if the participants are not necessarily part of the same command or organization - the product of successful unified action. There is no single template for achieving unity of effort.[30] While no one model exists for achieving unity of effort, past and present missions have tried a variety of different versions of the whole-of-government, comprehensive, and unified action approaches. The Provincial Reconstruction Teams (PRTs) may be the most recent and best-known platform for integrating multinational military and civilian efforts.

f. Military governance-support activities, tasks, and planning considerations are typically delegated to US Army and Marine Corps civil affairs (CA) forces, as well as planners of civil-military operations (CMO).[31] However, CA forces often are not available or present in sufficient numbers, or are not filling governance support or planning positions; as a result other military units may be responsible for planning, coordinating and executing governance support tasks in the immediate post-conflict period.

g. In most conflict settings, the UN often quickly organizes coordination groups, task forces, centers and other structures as part of current standard operations. The European Union, African Union, or other organizations may also build these coordination structures with attendance by donor representatives and implementing organizations and agencies present in theater. The JFC may establish civil-military operations centers (CMOC) as well.

h. Often coordination groups are formed to address problems in the immediate post-conflict period (e.g., humanitarian relief), but transition into other coordination fora as the mission evolves. In most environments, LOOs (such as demining, elections, internally displaced persons, rule of law, etc) will have its own multinational coordination task force or working group. In addition to sectoral and functional-based coordination

---

mechanisms, donors, IGOs, NGOs, foreign missions, and HN agencies will form internal, vertical coordination groups. Furthermore, horizontal coordination groups representing different staff levels may also form, such as the Principles Group, the Deputies Forum, or the USAID governance implementing partners.

KEY POINTS FOR PLANNERS

Plan to participate in these coordination and information-sharing mechanisms. If civilian organizations have yet to arrive or return, plan and staff governance and media development coordination mechanisms. Even if a CMOC is operating, do not expect that most organizations and donors will avail themselves of the Center to share plans and information. Find a location to meet outside the wire. Finally, there will be sensitivities about military-initiated coordination fora, so accept leadership by civilian partners as soon as those partners are capable, or have a civilian co-facilitator.

It is critical that the JFC and his or her staff plans and executes post-conflict US joint force assistance to support civilian agency reconstruction and development plans. The joint force may not have CA forces or CMO support. The most effective way to accomplish this goal is to establish partnerships with the Department of State political officers and with US Agency for International Development's OTI and DG officers.

Intentionally Blank

CHAPTER II
MILITARY SUPPORT TO POST-CONFLICT GOVERNANCE

"After three weeks of intense firefights, the Feydayeen Saddam fighters had finally slithered away. The last thing I expected to do once we entered Ar Rutbah, a Sunni city of about 25,000 in the Anbar province near Jordan and Syria, was to begin postwar reconstruction. I had not planned or prepared for governing, nor had I received any guidance or assistance in how to do so...."

LTC James A. Gavrillus
Foreign Policy
November/December 2005

1. Introduction

a. Post-conflict situations in countries present special challenges to the development of democratic and effective systems of governance. They call for a different planning and programming approach than might be used in a stable developing country. Societies emerging from conflict often have discredited or disintegrated systems of governance. If the same government continues in power from pre-conflict through the conflict, it is usually tainted because it failed to prevent the country from falling into conflict. If there is a new government, the administrative systems and bureaucracy left by the previous government tend to disintegrate as officials leave their posts, creating a vacuum of insecurity and incapacity. In Afghanistan, Iraq, and Kosovo, much of the government infrastructure ceased to exist in the wake of political settlements, and the legal and regulatory frameworks lost their relevance.[32]

b. This chapter presents guidance for JFCs and staffs on designing and developing plans to support democracy and governance (DG) programs in post-conflict reconstruction and stabilization situations. At the heart of this chapter are six individual lines of effort (LOEs) necessary to restore or reform governance. Each section lays out planning considerations related to that LOE. In addition to these LOE-specific planning considerations, there are task lists with illustrative activities that the JFC will need to anticipate and prepare to execute.

THE MILITARY PROBLEM

The joint force commander must develop the capability to support HN and International and USG governance-reconstruction and political development operations in order to enhance and increase stability, legitimacy, and effectiveness.

What military tasks to support post-conflict governance must joint force planners incorporate in campaign design?[33]

How can the military support the rapid and effective provision of services by sub-national units of government after cessation of hostilities?

---

2. Strategic, Policy, and Program End States

a. Governance programs should be planned and designed to achieve the larger US Government (USG) strategic objectives that initiated US involvement. These objectives flow from the *National Security Strategy*, the *National Defense Strategy*, and the *National Military Strategy* of the United States, as well as specific foreign policy objectives for the country and region in question.[34]

b. The end state for governance programs is a stable government that fulfills its core functions:

(1) delivering public goods and services effectively;

(2) managing political participation and accountability; and

(3) assuring security.

HOW CIVILIAN DEVELOPMENT AGENCIES APPROACH DEMOCRACY AND GOVERNANCE:

Excerpts From USAID's Democracy and Governance Program Goals for South and Central Asia During FY 2009[35]

The overarching aims of the United States in the region are to secure peace, advance development and strengthen democracy in Afghanistan; to build a stable, long-term relationship with Pakistan; to reinforce a firm partnership with India; and to advance democracy in South and Central Asia.

Regional Democracy & Governance (DG) Goals: As a new democracy, Afghanistan needs robust support, especially with presidential and parliamentary elections scheduled for 2009 and 2010. Funding also will support enhanced provincial and district-level governance and justice administration in order to improve service delivery, government responsiveness, transparency, and accountability. In Pakistan, the United States will intensify efforts to foster full democracy by building the political party system, local governance, and civil society capabilities, with an emphasis on expanded programs along the frontier with Afghanistan. Requested FY 2009 resources also will address extant and endemic corruption that hampers governance and economic development in Bangladesh, while supporting democratic openings in Nepal and Turkmenistan.

Afghanistan DG Goals: The top US priority is to build a government from the local to the national level that is responsive to the needs of the Afghan people. USAID assistance will strengthen nascent democratic institutions at the central, provincial, district, and local levels in order to help the Afghan government better serve the Afghan people and help them build a legitimate and capable state. FY 2009 funding also will support presidential, provincial council and parliamentary elections scheduled for 2009 -2010 by strengthening democratic political parties and other political entities such as the United Nations and Independent Electoral Commission..... Particular emphasis will be placed on strengthened sub-national governance functions such as the provision of public services. Finally, USAID will continue to support the strengthening of civil society, media, and freedom of information.

USAID Congressional Budget Justification for Foreign Operations, 2009

When these core functions are done well, citizens view the state as competent and legitimate. The box below offers an example of how broader US policy goals shape specific democracy and governance programs for the USAID in Afghanistan.

3. Conflict and Governance Assessments

CIVILIAN ASSESSMENTS OFFER IMPORTANT OPPORTUNITIES FOR PLANNERS

There are many types of assessments and a multitude of agencies and organizations that carry out governance assessments in a post-conflict environment. The assessment process is important for developing a clear understanding of the post-conflict environment and the development of programs. The military planner should be aware of the assessments being conducted by civilian agencies and should seek to leverage such assessments with their own military assessments.

FM 3-07, Appendix D

a. An **initial assessment** is usually the starting point for the process of re-establishing governance. According to FM 3-07, assessment is the process of surveying and analyzing a defined set of conditions in a comprehensive way.[36] Assessment in the development world refers holistically to the process of consultation, information gathering, and analysis as well as to the product of that process. Of the several military definitions of assessment, the one contained in JP 3-0—the continuous monitoring and evaluation of the current situation and progress of an operation—comes closest to civilian agency usage. In addition, there may be different kinds of assessments, depending on local conditions and the availability of resources available.

b. **Monitoring** provides a method for the in-process tracking of specific management information and performance indicators. If interventions produce results that are sub-optimal or widely diverging from those desired, this should trigger a more comprehensive evaluation of the situation. Causes of poor performance may include unintended consequences that need to be addressed, a change in conditions that require revisions to policy and/or program design, or assumptions underlying strategic choices that are no longer valid due to changing conditions.

c. Similarly, while **evaluation** in joint doctrine (JP 1-02) is defined as an intelligence appraisal, an item of information in terms of credibility, reliability, pertinence, and accuracy, the handbook reflects civilian agency usage in which evaluation refers to the process of determining the progress toward accomplishing a task, creating an effect, or achieving an objective. It may be undertaken as a formative, in-process or midterm evaluation, for the purpose of reconfirming or redirecting strategy and program design. It may also be conducted at the end of a program as a means of collecting and documenting lessons learned, or as input to the design of a new phase of interventions or operation.

4. USAID's Post-Conflict Assessment Process[37]

a. The key democracy and governance assessment process that the joint force is likely to support during contingency operations is USAID's democracy and governance assessment. An in-depth analysis of the conflict, as well as a survey of the democracy and governance dynamics, is vital to the development of USAID's strategy and program design. USAID is now refining a two-step process for a democracy and governance assessment. The first step is an in-depth assessment of the conflict using the Interagency Conflict Assessment Framework (ICAF). This is followed by and incorporated into the USAID Democracy and Governance (DG) Assessment Framework.

b. **Step One – ICAF**

(1) The ICAF, approved by the National Security Council's Reconstruction and Stabilization Interagency Coordinating Committee in 2008, was established to be the first step in any interagency planning process to assist in the establishment of USG goals, to design or reshape activities, to implement or revise programs, and to allocate or re-allocate resources.[38] ICAF provides a way of understanding the dynamics driving and mitigating conflict in a country, and should ideally precede a more focused sectoral assessment. ICAF is relatively an untested tool, as it was only adopted in 2008.

(2) ICAF is both an approach to understanding and transforming conflict and an interagency process that develops a common understanding of the problems. The three required steps for an ICAF review are:

(a) **Step 1: Examination of the Conflict's Context.** Identify the underlying (often longstanding) causes, their scope and duration, the nature of the conflict's settlement or suppression, and the role(s) of outsiders.

(b) **Step 2: Articulation of Core Grievances and Identification of Sources of Social and Institutional Fragility or Resilience.** Record the primary grievances of primary identity groups. What societal patterns and aspects of institutional performance contribute to volatility versus those that contribute to stabilization?

(c) **Step 3: Identification of Drivers of Conflict and Mitigating Factors.** Who are the leaders of key constituencies that can redirect social and institutional factors towards promotion of stability?

c. The figure below displays ICAF's key elements, their relationship, and the ordering of the assessment process.

d. If time prior to intervention permits, the findings of this broader analysis can be fed into the more focused *USAID Democracy and Governance (DG) Assessment Framework* to produce input into a democracy and governance strategic plan for the HN.

e. **Step Two – USAID Democracy and Governance Assessment.** USAID missions in the field are responsible for developing and submitting strategic plans for their use of program funds for democracy and governance. The DG assessment framework can be summarized in four stages:[39]

(1) **Stage 1: Define the Democracy and Governance (DG) Problems**. This analysis covers any weaknesses affecting stability in the five basic variables:

(a) **Extent of consensus** among key participants on national identity, rules of the political system and governing arrangements.

(b) **Status of the rule of law** needed to build state resilience, and establish the law and order needed for state legitimacy and effectiveness.

(c) **Structure of political and economic competition**, and the extent to which it is stabilizing (*e.g.*, by allowing for political power-sharing and an economic social safety net) or destabilizing (by causing some interests or groups to fail and thus opt out).

(d) **Extent of inclusion** of previously excluded or disadvantaged groups versus risk of paralysis due to polarization.

(e) **Good (or at least "good enough") governance** measured in terms of effectiveness in management of public goods and delivery of security and other public services.

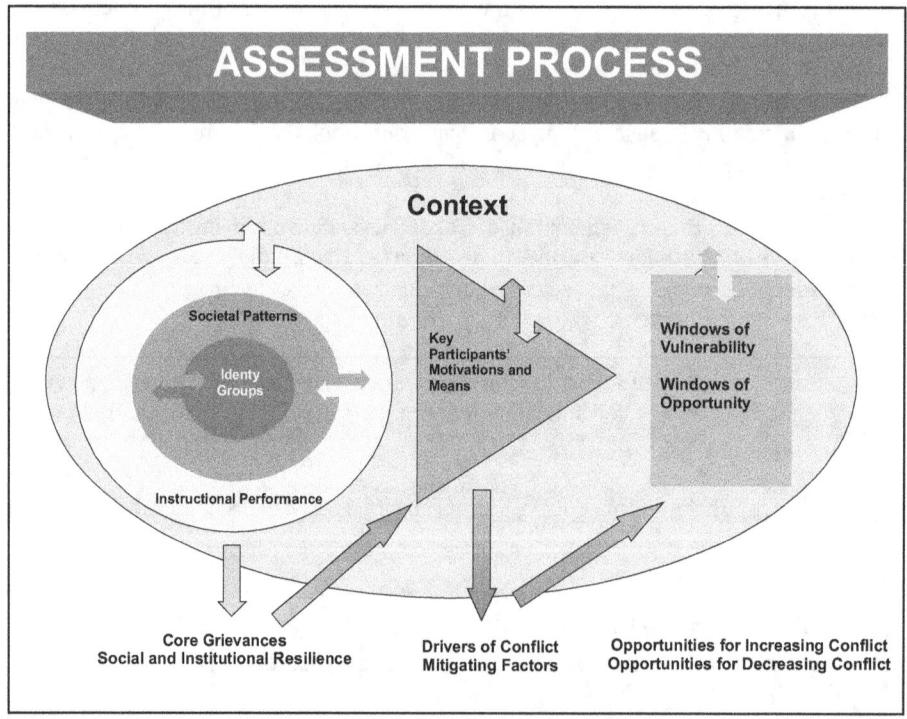

Figure II-1. Assessment Process

KEY QUESTIONS FOR A DG ASSESSMENT

Consensus: To what extent is there consensus on the fundamental rules of the political system, and to what extent is the political contest played according to those rules?

Competition: To what extent does meaningful competition take place in the political system and in other arenas of society? To what extent are there elections, a competition of ideas, a free media, and a vibrant civil society? Are meaningful checks and balances present in government? Is competition allowed and institutionalized? Are competitive arenas accessible? Is the competition fair? Is the political contest formalized, routine, and regulated by publicly accepted rules and norms?

Inclusion: Are there problems of inclusion and exclusion? Are parts of the population formally excluded and disenfranchised from meaningful political, social, or economic participation? Are there formal guarantees of inclusion?

Rule of law: Is there ordered liberty? Is politics, indeed are life, liberty, and property, bound by a rule of law? To what extent is the judicial system independent or free from political or other outside influence? To what extent do government bodies act in accordance with the law?

Governance: To what extent do social institutions (both in the public and private sectors), demonstrate a capacity to make and meet commitments, deliver reliably essential social services and be held accountable for their performance?

USAID,
Conducting A DG Assessment: A Framework for Strategy Development, 2000

(2) **Stage 2: Identify Key Political Participants and Their Allies**. A more specific analysis of the key individuals, interests, resources, and strategies leading to an understanding of how political processes are actually being played in the country.

(3) **Stage 3: Identify Key Institutions Central to Stability and Democratic Consolidation**. Conduct an analysis of the institutional arenas (legal, governmental and civil society). The four types of institutions that are candidates for examination include:

(a) **Law and the judiciary**.

(b) **Legislative and executive (including military) governance structures** and their authority, capacity, effectiveness, accountability and transparency.

(c) **Competitive structures** such as political parties, balance of powers among local and national levels and among branches of government, and the economy.

(d) **Civil society including media**.

(4) **Stage 4: Distill the Strategy**. Compare the problems identified above with the current diplomatic, defense and development activities (the three Ds), identify the gaps in resources and approaches, and propose possible programming response options that are compatible with available resources from the USG and other donors/contributors.

f. The first three steps generate a range of possible strategies for support or intervention. The fourth step analyzes the feasibility of putting these strategies in place. In effect, Steps 1 to 3 map possible routes and Step 4 determines which routes are feasible.[40]

USAID DG ASSESSMENT OF POLITICAL REFORM IN TANZANIA[41]

During a three week period in July 2003, a team of four consultants from ARD Inc and two officers from USAID's Center for Democracy and Governance conducted an assessment of Tanzania's transition from single–party rule to a country with formal democratic institutional structures. The assessment found that despite the legalization on opposition parties in 1992 and the first multiparty election in 1995, the previously dominant party, *Chama Cha Mapinduzi* (CCM) still exercised a de facto monopoly of political power and that the structures of the single-party state had not been transformed. The team recommended USAID support political reform by taking a "demand-driven" approach, *i.e.,* assisting in the development of a more effective and vocal civil society that can bring pressure to bear on political decision makers. The assessment suggested three broad areas of emphasis for USAID programs:

A demand-driven strategy coupled with creative opportunism in support for policy reform/advocacy initiatives;

Two primary institutional foci (civil society development and parliamentary strengthening); and

Two crosscutting themes (increased transparency and access to information, and anti-corruption).

Democracy and Governance Assessment of Tanzania: Transitions from a Single-Part State, Burlington, Vermont: ARD, Inc. November 2003

---

g. Data collection and analysis may involve a combination of research and interviews or focus group sessions with key country stakeholders. While the amount of time and resources required varies, research is typically conducted by a team of three people (USAID staff and consultants) over a period of approximately one month. More often than not, a DG assessment is conducted by one of USAID's contractors and grantees, such as Democracy International (DI), Management Systems International (MSI) or Creative Associates International Inc (CAII) with a USAID representative joining the assessment team.

5. Coordination of Assessments

a. A large challenge in today's complex operations is objectively assessing current governance capacities and obtaining broad-based participation in assessments.

Coordination across agencies, departments, contractors and international organizations and partners can be equally challenging.

USAID ASSESSMENT PARTNERS AND PROCESS

USAID normally contracts with a private organization to carry out it governance assessments in the field. Several organizations work closely with USAID on assessments, including Democracy International (DI), ARD Inc, and Management Services International (MSI). A typical assessment team might include four or five consultants from the USAID-funded contractor and one or two officers from USAID's Democracy Center. A team would probably spend about three weeks in the field collecting data and then perhaps two months analyzing and synthesizing its data. The final stage involves the preparation of the assessment report and its presentation to the local AID Mission and American Embassy. The entire assessment process would usually take three months.

USAID,
Conducting A DG Assessment: A Framework for Strategy Development

---

    b. The OECD DAC has established five guiding principles for enhanced impact, usage and harmonization of assessments:[42]

        (1) **Build on and strengthen nationally-driven governance assessments**. Donor assessments should draw on, and align with, the domestic assessment process within a country in order to drive the domestic dialogue on governance.

        (2) **Identify a clear key purpose to drive the choice of assessment tools and processes**. Assessments for an agency's internal purposes (e.g., programming) are not likely to be appropriate for purposes where country leadership and ownership are essential. In addition, having clear, limited and operational purposes will facilitate the choice of a relevant assessment tool and process and enhance their impact and use.

        (3) **Assess and address governance from different entry points and perspectives**. Every sector and thematic program features an element of governance which, to a greater or lesser extent, may be conducive to development. When targeted and jointly agreed upon and conducted, specific assessments are more likely to have an impact on shaping agendas in sectoral and thematic programs.

        (4) **Harmonize assessments at country level when the aim is to stimulate dialogue and governance reform**. When the primary purpose of assessments is to engage HN stakeholders, spark dialogue and encourage governance reform, multiple, uncoordinated assessments may be counterproductive. However, if assessments are primarily intended to serve internal agency purposes, the costs of harmonization may be greater than the benefits.

        (5) **Make results public unless there are compelling reasons not to release.**

SO MANY ASSESSMENTS – SO LITTLE COORDINATION: THE OECD'S 10 FINDINGS FROM WORK ON GOVERNANCE ASSESSMENTS[43]

A survey conducted by the Organization for Economic Co-operation and Development (OECD DAC) Network on Governance (GOVNET) highlighted the risks of duplication and overlap among donor assessment tools. Its findings:

1. There are strong incentives for individual donors to conduct their own assessments.

2. Examples of coordinated assessments are rare. The Rwanda Joint Governance Assessment is the only example to date of a fully coordinated national level assessment.

3. There are multiple definitions of governance and a multiplicity of assessment tools; the survey revealed the existence of 45 general methodologies, many of which overlap.

4. There is limited but growing donor interest in helping partner countries to diagnose their own governance challenges.

5. There is little donor interest in a single, unifying assessment tool, but scope to match the right tools for different purposes.

6. There are numerous opportunities for joint donor work and further harmonization in the field of assessment.

7. Transparency is a central concern and the disclosure of results must be carefully addressed in advance.

8. Joint assessments have the potential to improve the coherence of donor responses to corruption and weak governance.

9. The 2008 Accra Agenda for Action (AAA) may well place a new premium on high quality governance assessments to inform further action on aid predictability, the use of country systems and capacity development.

10. The "nation state" has been the predominant unit of analysis by donors to date, and much less attention is paid to international factors impacting on the quality of governance at the country level.

OECD "Donor Approaches to Governance Assessments: Guiding Principles for Enhanced Impact, Usage and Harmonisation," March 2009, p. 1

6. Assessment and Gender

Women and men often have different needs and interests in many areas of governance, and their experiences with institutions vary. It is therefore important to understand and take gender issues into account when assessing governance. However, most governance methodologies are gender-blind, and most data on governance cannot be disaggregated for gender. To capture different situations and experiences of women and men, indicators need to be constructed in a gender-sensitive, participatory manner to incorporate perspectives of both women and men. This includes indicator definition, data collection and analysis. Mainstream governance literature largely focuses on the need for more women in politics and decision making, especially in government. At the same time, a need exists to include a gender "lens" when looking at governance in other sectors, such as elections, media, justice and service delivery.

United Nations Development Programme (UNDP)'S GOVERNANCE ASSESSMENT PORTAL (GAP)

UNDP's Governance Assessment Portal (GAP) is a valuable resource for assessment planning. The portal holds links to a wide range of publications and governance assessment frameworks under categories such as "areas of governance" (*e.g.,* corruption, parliaments, justice); a "source guide to global indicators;" an "inventory of country initiatives" (country-led governance assessments); a "governance assessment library" (online publications on a range of approaches to governance assessments); "UNDP publications;" and a "toolbox" (stocked with assessment frameworks and indicators ready for use)

GAP is available at www.gaportal.org

---

7. USAID Planning

a. Just as DOD is developing approaches to reconstruction and stabilization, USAID's planning framework is in a state of development and no decisions have yet been made on how to proceed. Until further guidance becomes available, the following table provides an overview of USAID planning at the Mission (Embassy) level.

8. Military Tasks and Planning Considerations for Post-Conflict Governance and Participation

a. The DOS's Office of the Coordinator for Stabilization and Reconstruction (S/CRS) Essential Task Matrix (ETM) is an essential tool to integrate joint operational design into whole-of-government planning. It is a living document and available on the S/CRS website. The ETM was developed by six interagency working groups, led by S/CRS, and was based on the Center for Strategic and International Studies (CSIS)[44] work. The task framework catalogs the tasks for five technical sectors (security, humanitarian assistance and social well-being, economic stabilization and infrastructure, justice and reconciliation, and governance and participation.). A range of political development activities supported and funded by foreign assistance programs is organized under the sector known as "governance and participation."

b. The goals of the tasks in the ETM focus on institutions, processes, and behaviors necessary to rebuild government capacity; the mechanisms and processes for citizens, civil society and political party organizations to articulate their interests in the development of public policy; and the methods and rules for the selection and election of government leaders.

c. In post-conflict environments, prioritizing governance-support tasks is a critical. Not all governance support tasks can or should be undertaken in the initial and transitional phases of stabilization, nor will the sequence of interventions likely be the same in any two situations.

d. The following governance sub-sectors, or LOEs are essential building blocks for the establishment of a representative, participatory government and a society where power-sharing arrangements exist and conflict can be channeled into non-violent competition, the desired end state for conflicts.

(1) Interim and transitional national governance (to include ministerial-level support).

(2) Constitutional processes.

(3) Interim and transitional local governance (to include departmental-level support).

(4) Creating or strengthening of viable legislative processes.

(5) Creation or legitimization of a multiparty political system.

(6) Evolutionary development of civil society within regionally acceptable societal frameworks and norms.

e. The following sections provide the JFC and staff with a basic understanding of command responsibilities in creating or restoring government and political institutions immediately after conflict and in the transitional phase. The transitional phase is indefinite, and depends on the level of persistent violence, the emerging government's capacities and capabilities, and the political will of the United States and our allies.[45]

9. Constitutional Processes

a. The process of drafting and promulgating a constitution lays the foundation for post-conflict governance and is an integral part of peacemaking and stabilization. A broad-based participatory process in forming a new constitution is an especially important element in providing legitimacy to both to the constitution itself and a post-conflict government. Giving HN citizens ownership of the process defuses concerns about outside control or partisanship and may also promote reconciliation in the post-conflict period.

b. There may be powerful elites who want to maintain the status quo and oppose a consultative process. Although ruling elites cannot be ignored, their interests should be balanced against the need for broader public participation.

c. Although conditions vary from country to country, there are usually three phases of constitutional development:

(1) **Preparatory** – This phase involves initial negotiations on procedures, timelines, basic principles, possible adoption of an interim constitution, and the

FOREIGN ASSISTANCE PLANNING/PROGRAMMING DOCUMENTATION AT THE USAID MISSION LEVEL		
Documents	**Purpose**	**Frequency and Period Covered**
Joint State USAID Strategic Plan (Joint State USAID) Strategic Goals	Defines the primary aims of US foreign policy and development assistance as well as our strategic priorities within each of those goals.	Frequency: Every 5 years Period Covered: 5 years
Country Assistance Strategies (Joint USG) Strategic Goals Regional Priorities	Sets longer term country specific foreign assistance priorities and expected results. Jointly developed by Washington and field; final approval in Washington	Frequency: Every 5 years Period Covered: 5 years
	Sets longer term country specific foreign assistance priorities and expected results when no joint USG country assistance strategy is in place. Parameters are set by and strategy is approved by the respective regional bureau Assistance Administrator	Frequency: Every 5 years Period Covered: 5 years
Mission Strategic Plan (MSP) (Joint USG) Strategic Goals	Initiates USG strategic budgeting cycle for 150 account Reviewed/approved in Washington	Frequency: Annual Period Covered: 3 years
Operational Plan (Joint USG) Functional Objectives, Program Areas, Elements, Sub Elements	Proposes 1) budget allocation below the Program Area level and 2) means of implementation Budget, higher level narratives and key issue funding reviewed/approved in Washington	Frequency: Annual Period Covered: 1 year for budget and performance; 2 out years for performance targets
Regional and Sectoral Strategies (USAID) Strategic Goals, Priorities, Themes, Regional approaches.	Presents priorities for USAID's regional bureaus and sectors	Frequency: As needed Period Covered: As needed
*Assistance Objective Planning (USAID) Results Framework, Intermediate Results, Performance Management Plan, Statutory Checklists, Environmental Review	Supports a comprehensive set of projects and activities that will achieve a specific AO within funding parameters. Internal to USAID Mission	Frequency: Every 3 5 years Period Covered: 3 5 years
Activity Approval Document (USAID)	Documents compliance with project and activity design requirements. Internal to USAID Mission	Frequency: Every 2 5 years Period Covered: 2 5 years

Table II-1. Foreign Assistance Planning/Programming Documentation at the USAID Mission Level

establishment of a body to draft the constitution. Initial public information and consultations are also part of this phase.

(2) **Drafting** – Extensive consultations with legal experts and advisors, a broad range of stakeholders, political parties, and the public are part of a national dialogue during in this phase. The end product is a draft constitution prepared through a transparent drafting process.

(3) **Review and Adoption** – The draft constitution is now put before the public through an information campaign and reviewed by existing governmental bodies (e.g., legislature, courts, and constitutional assembly) and the public. After modification of the draft in response to expert and public comment, there will be a process to formally adopt the constitution, possibly through a public referendum. Public education on the new constitution follows.

d. In a post-conflict situation, constitutional development is central to establishing a new institutional structure and forging a sense of national identify. In a deeply divided society, however, this may reignite conflict rather than alleviate it. In these situations a piecemeal approach, using an interim constitution and extending the formal constitutional process by postponement of direct engagement with controversial issues may be necessary.

EXAMPLE – CONSTITUTION IN POST-CONFLICT EAST TIMOR[46]

In East Timor the National Democratic Institute for International Affairs (NDI) conducted focus group surveys immediately after the end of armed conflict. Trained moderators met with small groups of citizens to discuss their expectations for peace and priorities for development. These discussions provided important insights into the views of the population that contributed to the drafting of the constitution. One of the points emphasized by East Timorese was their strong desire to protect basic civil rights, which was incorporated into the new constitution.

Shari Bryan, "Engaging Political Parties in Post-Conflict Parliaments," International Conference on Parliaments, Crisis Prevention and Recovery, Brussels, Belgium, April 19-20, 2006.

---

e. **Military Tasks**

(1) Offer military assistance to the AMEMB Country Team, in particular the political section and the USAID democracy and governance officer, who are involved in the constitutional process.

(2) Provide legal expertise to drafters, as requested, especially in the area of the security sector.

(3) Provide security, in support of local forces, to meeting sites for drafters, public fora for discussions, and a nationwide constitutional referendum.

(4) Provide logistic support, if required (e.g., transporting members of the drafting committee for public consultations around the country).

f. **Military Planning Considerations**

(1) **The military's role in constitutional development will probably be focused on logistics, security and the provision of legal expertise.** Essentially the joint force will support, as appropriate, USG and international agencies. In order to play a constructive role, it will be important to have personnel with legal experience or knowledge of constitutional structures for managing defense and security sector issues.

(2) **The military should ensure that US and international agencies supporting constitutional development address defense and security affairs.** Military expertise may provide counsel concerning the design of mechanisms for civilian oversight.

(3) **Basic rules governing the constitutional development process should be established at the outset of the process.** The rules should enable a robust process of public engagement and should protect fundamental rights of the population.

(4) **In a presidential system, strengthening the legislature as a check on excessive executive power should be a factor in constitutional development.** In post-conflict situations legislatures are usually weak and ineffective compared with the executive branch. In developing a constitution, joint force advisors and planners should encourage interagency partners, coalition members, IGOs, NGOs, and international donors to consider ways to structure a more balanced government, including measures such as including presidential term limits.

(5) **Public participation in constitutional development requires social inclusion, personal security, and freedom of speech and assembly.**

10. Interim and Transitional National Governance

a. The bulk of the responsibility for supporting governance in areas not related to security and logistics will generally fall to the DOS, USAID and the Department of Justice, as well as coalition members and other donor governments, international organizations, and nongovernmental organizations (NGOs). However, the joint force may need to be prepared to handle these tasks if civilian agencies are unable to operate effectively due to a hostile or uncertain security environment.

b. Where US military forces may be among the first international components to arrive in a failing or failed state, their tasks under this line of effort may include assuming temporary responsibility for providing government services until either interim international civilian administrators can be mobilized or until the HN government itself is strong enough to assume these responsibilities.

PLANNING LESSONS AND FAILED STATE INTERVENTIONS

Establishing and supporting effective transitional governance is one of the most formidable challenges facing reconstruction and stabilization missions in failed states. The experience of international interventions in failed states since the early 1990s demonstrates that governance is not a mission that intervening parties can postpone or ignore without jeopardizing the objectives of the intervention. The failed state interventions of the 1990s offer two essential lessons:

(1) International interventions cannot secure a lasting peace unless they lead to functioning institutions of governance guided by accountable leaders with the support of the governed population.

(2) Interventions in failed states have a short window of opportunity – typically about six months – to develop effective public institutions and programs, so success is impossible without intensive pre-deployment planning for governance support.

VARIOUS SOURCES, to include USIP, UNDP and USAID

c. **Military Tasks**

(1) **Initial or "first-response" tasks** may include:

(a) Based on an assessment of existing HN capability and capacity, work with the country team and other USG and international partners to determine the need for first response governance, identifying unmet institutional needs, prioritizing government functions, and reestablishing government services

(b) Protect key government leaders, ministry buildings, and other facilities until HN security forces are capable;

(c) Conduct emergency repairs to enable key government buildings and facilities to resume functioning;

(2) **Transition tasks** for military forces may include:

(a) Support establishment of transitional political authority to include recommending leaders for the new administration, if necessary.

(b) Provide military insight on the establishment of an interim national government. Proposed rules or timetables that would be established for an interim or transitional government.

(c) Participate in vetting proposed security sector appointees to transitional or interim government positions to guard against appointment of individuals involved in corruption, war crimes or serious human rights abuses, and other problems that could disqualify them from service.

(d) Assist the country team and the transitional government with public communications activities to keep citizens apprised of progress or manage expectations.

(e) Provide logistic support to key transitional government and other national-level leaders.

"The U.S.-led coalition that invaded Iraq, toppled Saddam Hussein's regime, and occupied the country for thirteen months attempted to build the foundations of democratic governance .. The coalition's initial plan—to remove Saddam and his close associates from power and to hold in place the existing bureaucracy to administer the country—became untenable when those structures dissolved. Looters gutted seventeen of twenty-three ministries, stealing or destroying their records, while ministry personnel went home or disappeared. When the initial plan proved unrealizable, there was, by all accounts, no backup strategy. As a consequence, several independent and uncoordinated streams of activity to create governance structures got under way; the ad hoc nature of the ensuing process and the lack of coordination and shared objective"[47]

Celeste J. Ward, The Coalition Provisional Authority's Experience with Governance in Iraq: Lessons Identified, Special Report No. 139, US Institute for Peace, Washington, DC, May 2005.

d. **Planning Considerations**

(1) **Military forces should be prepared conduct a broad large range of governance activities that are normally handled by civilians.** This will be particularly true in the days immediately following combat operations or when a hostile or uncertain security environment limits the ability of civilians to govern.

(2) **As a part of operational design[48], joint planners should conduct a predeployment governance assessment in coordination with civilian agencies.** Early assessment of national government capabilities is critical to establishing initial government authority and restoring essential government services. In addition to estimating the likely capability of a transitional government to provide essential services, the assessment should include the cultural, political, economic, historical, and technological characteristics that define the society. It should also identify crucial humanitarian, security and development needs, any continuing sources of violent conflict, and the nature of informal power structures likely to obstruct the creation or restoration of order and effective governance. Governance elements in operational design should consider all sources of trade, production and income generation in the region, to include valid activities, such as farming, mining and industrial production, and illicit activities, such as drug production and distribution, human trafficking and extortion, in order to develop strategies to encourage valid activities, while simultaneously discouraging illicit activities.

(3) **Embed governance advisors in the joint force prior to deployment to advise critical first response governance decisions.** Forward deployed governance advisors

will assist the JFC and his staff identify potential "spoilers" to the development of governance in each locality and region in the operational area.

(4) **The JFC should ensure that the mandate for transitional governance under international authority clearly defines the relationship between civilian and military authorities and their respective areas of competence.** The simplest structure combines military and civilian authorities in a single entity, such as the Office of the High Representative in Bosnia or the Coalition Provisional Authority in Iraq. Other structures in recent conflicts, such as Kosovo and East Timor, have assigned responsibility for military operations to NATO or a multinational force and control of civilian tasks to the United Nations.

(5) **Commanders should give priority to restoring basic public services disrupted by conflict.** Governments are generally expected to provide basic public services, including state-run education, public health care, and the construction and maintenance of roads. During conflict, provision of these services may be interrupted or shut off. Restoring such services serves multiple objectives, including signaling to the populace that the conflict is over and that conditions are improving. The wages paid to teachers, doctors and nurses, and other government employees help restart local economies and avoid personal economic hardship.

(6) **If a new governing structure needs to be established, international authorities should incorporate legitimate components of the existing governance and bureaucratic structure in the first response administration.** There are three basic models for incorporating HN leaders in a first response administration: 1) a political advisory council composed of leaders who provide advice to the transitional government; 2) a joint military committee made up of high-ranking military commanders from various factions who provide counsel regarding military and security questions; and 3) a joint functional committee composed of civilians from a variety of sectors—for example, health care, communication services, and education—who provide advice and oversee administration functions.

(7) **Find Ways to Limit Purely Political Appointments.** International authorities should weigh the benefits of appointing warlords or other prominent political figures to key positions in a post-conflict government in order to keep the peace against the merits of appointing persons who are more technically qualified for office. If political appointments of unqualified persons are truly necessary, it may be possible to reduce the damage by limiting the term of office of appointees and pairing elite but unqualified appointees with competent staff.

(8) **Understand International Civilian Agency Programming Plans.** Joint planners should maintain awareness of assessments and plans of other coalition members, as well as members of the international community; such as foreign donor governments, IGOs and other international organizations, and NGOs; to help reestablish effective governance in the HN.

(9) **Provide force commanders with sufficient resources to quickly set up ministries and other key government institutions.** The "ministry-in-a-box" concept,

first implemented by the UN in Afghanistan and used again by USAID's Office of Transition Initiatives in Iraq, is a possible approach to rapidly restore post-conflict government ministries that have been totally destroyed. A "ministry-in-a-box" includes items ranging from paint and basic office supplies to more sophisticated mail and computer operations, to jumpstart ministry operations.

THE IRAQ "MINISTRIES-IN-A-BOX" EXPERIENCE[49]

To help restart looted and broken ministries in Baghdad, USAID contractor Development Alternatives Incorporated (DAI) created a package called "ministry-in-a-box." Each kit cost $122,000 and provided furniture and supplies for 100 civil servants. USAID employed dozens of small Iraqi companies to manufacture and assemble all the elements that went into the each package. The ministries soon demanded more kits, and DAI had delivered a total of 132 "ministries-in-a-box" by the fall of 2003.

Various USAID Reports

---

(10) **Provide JFCs with financial resources to immediately pay essential civil service workers such as teachers, police, medial personnel, and local and national administrators.**

(11) **Assess the need for the transitional government programs to collect and manage revenue and support their implementation, while simultaneously building transparent and accountable budget processes.** Widespread corruption is only possible because of poor oversight and lack of transparency and accountability. As government revenues increase, corruption, lack of transparency and lack of accountability will also increase in the absence of proper governance development.

(12) **Establish advisory councils and other mechanisms for local input or administration as early as possible.** Such councils and mechanisms should aim not only to ensure local policy input, but to help build local governance capacity. If the country is not yet fully self-governing, local participation may be facilitated through consultative mechanisms or co-administration. Whichever mechanism is used, local participation should be encouraged as early as possible following the intervention.

(13) **Make Conflict-Sensitive Personnel Decisions.** Military commanders involved in selecting HN personnel to fill positions in a first response or transitional government should understand that their decisions will confer power and money to the people they select. This applies not only to choosing key government personnel, but to the selection of teachers, health workers, and police officers. Commanders should ensure that their choices do not exacerbate existing tensions by drawing heavily on members of one ethnic group or tribe while excluding others.

11. Interim and Transitional Local Governance

a. In this section, provincial, municipal and other local levels are collectively referred to as local governance. The bulk of the responsibility for supporting local governance in areas not related to security, logistics, and public communications will generally fall to civilian USG agencies, international organizations, and nongovernmental organizations (NGOs). However, the joint force must handle these tasks if civilian agencies are unable to operate or to operate effectively due to a hostile or uncertain security environment.

> **THE NATIONAL CONSULTATIVE COUNCIL DURING UN TRANSITIONAL ADMINISTRATION IN TIMOR LESTE (EAST TIMOR)[50]**
>
> **The UN Transitional Administration in Timor-Leste (UNTAET) created the National Consultative Council to serve as a consultative body. The Council was composed of 15 members; including representatives of the National Council of Timorese Resistance, the Catholic Church, pro-autonomy groups, and UNTAET itself. Although one pro-autonomy group refused to join the NCC, the council was able to serve as a fairly effective forum for local participation in the international administration. In addition, because the NCC was largely representative, it helped to confer legitimacy on the international administration.**
>
> **Beth Cole DeGrasse and Cristina Caan. Transitional Governance, From Bullets to Ballots, Washington, DC, US Institute of Peace, July 2006**

b. In fragile post-conflict states, rapid and substantial improvements in subnational public services can be important in averting or ameliorating humanitarian disasters and giving disenfranchised groups incentive to engage in politics rather than violence. Establishing more democratic and decentralized local governing structures can in turn help to make local government levels responsive to individual and local community interests and therefore potentially more effective, both politically and in terms of the value placed on local government services by the public. In addition to building political support for provincial and local levels in government, restoring local government bodies can encourage the population to cooperate with authorities in suppressing an insurgency.

c. Often in a post-conflict environment, responsibility for providing government services may have, for all practical purposes, devolved from the central to local governments as a result of the central government's inability to provide such services or because governance was based on a weak central state model. In some failed states, there may be no government to support. In these cases, reconstituting provincial and local governments and helping them to provide services can reduce the risk that the absence or inadequacy of services will exacerbate tensions between groups or trigger renewed conflict.

d. Building capacity at the local level of government can involve providing technical assistance to expand both local government's ability to provide services as well as to make policy. The need to strengthen the capacity of provincial and local levels of governments may be acute if the peace agreement or other negotiated settlement ending the conflict provides for greater regional autonomy within a federated state, as was the case in Bosnia and

Herzegovina, or for outright independence. According to USAID's handbook for local government programming, building local government capacity to develop policy can include technical assistance and training linked to standard processes to include:[51]

(1) financial policies associated with the local government budget;

(2) procurement policy associated with contracting for and purchasing of goods and supplies;

(3) policies governing access to public records;

(4) open meetings and open records policies;

(5) public notification policies, particularly those related to land use and community planning; and

(6) personnel policies associated with professional development of local government employees.

e. **Military Tasks**

(1) **Initial or "First-Response"** military tasks may include:

(a) Provide first response governance to deliver essential and critical government services.

(b) Identify leaders at the provincial and local levels of government and establish contact.

(c) Determine who has the lead for public communication and support as required.

(d) Protect provincial and local government leaders and facilities until HN security forces are capable.

LESSONS FROM THE FIELD: "FIRST RESPONSE GOVERNANCE"[52]

Security and governance are inseparable. Quickly close the basic security and governance gap associated with combat operations. This gap is fertile ground for insurgents.

Retain a monopoly on the use of force, even though incoming US joint and coalition forces may perform other roles.

Disarm former combatants and potential combatants quickly. Go after guns and munitions but do not go after individuals or groups unless they insist on continuing the fight.

Quickly establish an effective security force and avoid any hint of the former regime's oppressive tactics in the provision of security.

Rapidly involve and integrate with HN local police. It will engender trust and cooperation. They are critical for restoring local security. Be mindful, however, that the local police you need today may be the ones culled tomorrow as the focus shifts from immediate security to rooting out corruption.

Elect, select or appoint decisions makers from the community ASAP. Establish a process of selecting interim mayors and political leaders – BUT be sure not to play favorites. Be mindful that ethic, tribal and political elites will try to manipulate an early selection process. Do not be a stooge.

Creating some kind of public "pledging" ceremony where newly selected police, mayors, councilors, and other public leaders renounce their old ways and affirm their loyalty and allegiance to the country and its people. This commits the leaders publicly, builds citizens' confidence, and endows a legitimacy to the process.

Meet with interim leaders to establish government service priorities promptly. Work day and night if restoration of electricity, water, or garbage clean-up are priorities for the community. Focus on quick, practical and visible results.

Involve citizens in the post-conflict cleanup. Typically, initial military forces are limited in number and can't do it all. Nor should they. Including citizens in the restoration of their communities sends powerful messages of ownership, responsibility, opportunity, and new beginnings. But care must be exercised that they not be perceived as working for or "agents" of the US.

Post-conflict stability is more than just policing the streets and turning on the lights. Contribute to establishing an environment whereby people to use their own ingenuity and relationships to get food into the market, the gas stations working, the banks, mosques, temples and churches opened.

Ensure that the interim mayor or city manager has some financial resources to restore government services. Plan to provide some of those resources using it as an opportunity to develop a quick budget. This is also a great opportunity to begin holding local officials accountable and to make the process transparent to citizens.

Be prepared to spend some money, but money will not cure the security or governance challenges. Good leadership, evident results and visible security are worth than money.

An interim authority may be autocratic by necessity to quickly set boundaries and establish a system of governance. But take measures to avoid the immediate post-conflict authority eroding into longer-term dictatorship.

Support any democratic inclinations by the people. It may be a jirga, a simple election, a town caucus or other means in which citizens can have a say in the selection of leaders. The particular form of governance may not be as important as providing opportunities for citizens to participate in the new community order – particularly if they have survived years of oppression or conflict.

Find opportunities for members of other leadership and political elites to participate in the new government, even though they may not hold a "selected" or "elected" role. It will build trust and keeps them inside the tent, instead of inciting discord from the margins.

As soon as capable people are in place, pass any decision-making that you have assumed on to them. You should not be the focal point of governance.

Do not occupy homes or former regime buildings. Live modestly, not like conquering kings.

Be prepared to perform a wide variety of tasks under direction of civilian authority depending on the needs on the ground.

Work with and through the local population and treat them as allies, not enemies.

Recognize that security, economics and governance are interdependent. Governing – as least in the short-term – is your job.

Adapted from *The Mayor of Ar Rutbah* (*FP* Nov/Dec 2005)
James A. Gavrillus, US Army Special Forces (Ret)

(2) **Transitional military tasks** may include:

(a) Provide support to interim provincial and local government leaders.

(b) Participate in vetting proposed appointees to provincial and local government positions to prevent selection of individuals involved in corruption, war crimes or human rights abuses, and other problems.

(c) Provide strategic communication support to provincial and local governments.

(d) Support establishment of a liaison process between local and national-level government authorities and institutions.

(e) In cooperation with other USG agencies, particularly USAID and its contractors and other international donors, identify deficiencies in local government operations and services and work with provincial and local authorities to build the necessary government capacities.

RESTORING LOCAL GOVERNANCE IN POST-WAR IRAQ

After the coalition's military victory, Iraq was divided into six major subordinate commands (MSCs): north, north-central, western, Baghdad, center-south, and southeast. MSC commanders were charged with securing their sectors and beginning reconstruction. To carry out their mission, military units needed Iraqi interlocutors and thus began to build local and regional councils. The MSCs drew from three sources of funding to initiate reconstruction projects—the Development Fund for Iraq (DFI), Iraqi assets from oil exports and other income sources, and the Commanders Emergency Response Program (CERP) under which brigade commanders could disburse up to $100,000 and division commanders up to $500,000 without consulting higher authorities.

According a study by the US Institute for Peace (USIP)[53], evidence suggests that military units received only very general guidance about how to carry out post-combat missions. In the absence of preplanning or guidance, commanders were left to freelance, making it up as they went along, and joint forces did not have a shared understanding of Coalition or National Strategic Objectives. The study noted that the May 2003 establishment of a provincial council in Ninawah Province, which also served as the city council for Mosul, was a positive example of military efforts to create local governance. The Ninawah Province council was established by Major General David Petraeus, then the commander of the 101st Airborne. Illustrating the potential size and complexity of local governance operations, the USIP study cited April 2003 USAID contracts, potentially worth $236 million over two years, to the Research Triangle Institute (RTI), a nonprofit organization experienced in the development of government institutions. Without coordinating with the Office of Reconstruction and Humanitarian Assistance (ORHA), the CPA, or the MSCs, RTI began its mission in late April, when it started work in Basra. By the time RTI arrived, British coalition forces had set up a city council there. RTI soon relocated a substantial part of its effort to Baghdad, where it helped to establish councils at the neighborhood and district levels and eventually a city and a provincial council.

In Baghdad, RTI, the CPA, and the military's civil military operations center (CMOC) began to establish local governance, stetting up eighty-eight neighborhood advisory councils, nine district advisory councils, and a city advisory council. Iraqis elected the neighborhood advisory councils (in some cases they were appointed), which voted on representatives to the district advisory council. In turn, these council members voted on representatives to the city advisory council.

With the success of the Baghdad process, the CPA sought to replicate this model throughout Iraq, assigning small governance teams to all fifteen of the non-Kurdish provinces. Although the teams' composition varied, they generally included a CPA provincial coordinator and a deputy, as well as military personnel and staff from RTI. Teams arriving in the provinces found a variety of governing structures that had already been created by the military. They worked with these structures and created new councils where needed. Not surprisingly, the composition and procedures of these councils varied widely, as did their legitimacy among Iraqis. Over time, the CPA appointed regional coordinators to oversee activities in broad sections of the country. Significantly, the CPA divided the country into four administrative regions—north, central/Baghdad, south-central, and south—that did not correspond to the military's six MSCs.

Celeste J. Ward, The Coalition Provisional Authority's Experience with Governance in Iraq: Lessons Identified, Special Report No. 139, US Institute for Peace,
Washington, DC, May 2005

f. Military Planning Considerations

(1) Due to resource constraints, it may be necessary to work directly with a limited number of local governments on a pilot-project basis, then disseminate information on innovations or replicate successful activities in other localities.

(2) If the former government exercised strong centralized control over the country, in coordination with appropriate US civilian and international authorities, it may be necessary to provide assistance to members of the national legislature with the drafting of laws that give local governments more authority and access to revenue than they previously enjoyed.

(3) Commanders should encourage the establishment of municipal associations, which in turn can help design and promote legislative proposals for reforms involving local government. Municipal associations can also help to represent the concerns of local communities at the national level and act as a political counterweight to the central government.

(4) Commanders should encourage local and provincial governments to adopt procedures that give citizens a voice on security sector reform and other major local government decisions. One way governments can encourage citizen involvement is to improve public access to local government information.

(5) Program managers should look for ways to elicit citizen input when making decisions on assisting local governance. Assistance programs should be implemented in ways that help empower citizens and make local governments more participatory, more accountable, and, consequently, more effective. This helps ensure that governance at the local level becomes increasingly democratic and facilitates the transition to democracy at the national level. Managers can promote citizen input into decision-making through consultative mechanisms such as task forces, advisory committees, town meetings, public hearings and opinion polls. The mechanisms selected should be based on local cultural and practices. In some cases, it may be possible to employ a traditional consultative mechanism that has fallen into disuse because it was discouraged by an authoritarian central government.

(6) Training officials in strategic and financial planning is critical to building local and provincial government capacity.

(7) Local program managers can have an impact at a national level by widely publicizing success in local-level governance programs and activities.

(8) Previously oppressed, disenfranchised, or under-represented groups— such as women, ethnic groups, and other minorities — should be actively encouraged to participate in local government.

CREATING A NEW LEGAL FRAMEWORK FOR LOCAL GOVERNMENT IN POLAND[54]

Efforts to decentralize government in Poland during the transition from communist rule in the 1990s required establishing a new legal basis for local government. To this end, USAID provided advisors on local government finance law, who worked with the Ministry of Finance and national municipal associations, providing them advice and policy analysis. The program helped the associations to play a role in the debates over fiscal decentralization and helped lead to legislation in 1998 that redefined the budgets and revenue bases for both national and local governments. The legislation granted local governments increased access to capital for investment and allowed them to receive greater revenue from the national government and local tax collection authority. This in turn permitted local governments to take on new responsibilities for delivering services and managing resources.

USAID's Experience in Decentralization and Democratic Local Governance,
USAID Center for Democracy and Development,
Washington, DC, September 2000

---

12. Creating or Strengthening Viable Legislative Processes

a. Strengthening legislative institutions can contribute to post-conflict reconstruction and stabilization by providing a forum for competing segments of society to resolve contentious issues, while at the same time fostering the growth of representative democracy. Legislatures can also check the growth of excessive power by the executive or a dominant political party and serve as a forum for alternative political views and platforms.

b. Nonetheless, legislatures may not be ideal for conflict resolution and reconciliation and are not well suited for negotiating peace agreements. Reflecting the divisions in society, legislatures may in fact exacerbate tensions and if there is not tradition of toleration of minorities, they can be an instrument for suppression of groups or marginalization of the political opposition. In a post-conflict situation, legislative institutions often are weak in relation to the executive, the military, armed groups and non-state organizations. There are often few talented and experienced people to serve in a legislature as well as a shortage of qualified staff. In addition, lack of physical and financial resources may be a problem. Finally, there may be unrealistically high public expectations for a new legislature that can lead to disillusionment if the new institution is unable to perform as expected.

c. There is often a delay in establishing a legislature, giving the executive an advantage in terms of power, authority, donor attention, resources, personnel and experience. In addition, the executive will probably promulgate laws in the interim that may weaken the legislature's role once it is operational. Early elections for the legislature can help correct the imbalance, but if held too early other problems may arise. An inexperienced, inadequately resourced parliament could become either a rubber stamp or ineffectual, undermining public support of the institution. Creating a broadly representative interim legislature, strengthening it as soon as possible after the end of the conflict, and planning for long-term support can help address some of these problems.

d. Using a system of proportional representation, under which candidates or parties in a multi-member electoral district are selected in proportion to their share of the vote, can result in broader representation in the legislature and can moderate tensions in the society. On the other hand, weak coalitions or minority governments may result, leading to instability, frequent elections, and increased public disenchantment from the political process. Majoritarian or "first-past-the-post" systems are used in single-member districts where voters elect the one candidate or party receiving the most votes. This system usually results in more stability but also limits the number of political parties that can survive. It may result in narrower representation in the legislature, and can stifle dissent. Regardless of the system, a diverse and proportionate parliament can have a moderating effect in a post-conflict environment.

e. Legislatures have an important role to play in oversight of the state's security sector. The committee structure of the legislature should include a defense committee that helps bring security under civilian control. It should offer advice and make recommendations to the full legislature on issues of national defense and the security of the nation's citizens. A defense committee, however, differs in several ways from other parliamentary committees:

(1) **Complexity of Issues**. The committee must consider a wide range of institutions and issues (e.g., the armed forces, police, border security, budgets, procurement, arms control, and intelligence oversight). These often have an international component.

(2) **Limited Transparency**. Many of the institutions and issues the committee must handle are sensitive or classified because of national security implications. This can be a source of tension in the legislature and between the legislature and the security sector.

(3) **Strong Involvement of the Executive**. The executive branch usually plays the dominant role in defense and security issues and may bypass the legislature in dealing with other nations.

(4) **Weak Involvement of Civil Society**. In many countries there are no NGOs dealing with the security sector and the public is not well informed about the issues.[55]

f. The roles and responsibilities of a defense committee, which usually must work with other committees (e.g., intelligence, foreign affairs, home affairs, budget and possibly others) include:

(1) Legislation for the defense and security sector.

(2) Advise on budgets and monitor expenditures.

(3) Review government defense policy and security strategy.

(4) Consult on international commitments and treaties to be ratified by the legislature.

(5) Advise on the use of force and the deployment of troops abroad.

(6) Monitor defense procurement.[56]

(7) Exercise broad oversight through:

 (a) hearings or inquiries;

 (b) summoning military personnel, civil servants or experts to committee meetings to testify;

 (c) questioning ministers and other executive representatives;

 (d) requesting documents from the executive;

 (e) scrutinizing the transparency and efficiency of public spending;

 (f) requesting the competent authorities to perform audits;

 (g) examining petitions and complaints from military personnel and civilians concerning the defense and security sector; and

 (h) visiting and inspecting army bases and other premises of security services, including troops deployed abroad.[57]

g. The primary USG agency involved in legislative development is USAID, which often works through the International Republican Institute (IRI) and the National Democratic Institute for International Affairs (NDI). The joint planner will also find a wide range of international agencies and NGOs engaged in projects to strengthen legislatures. These include the United Nations Development Programme (UNDP),[58] the Organization for Security Cooperation in Europe (OSCE), and NGOs such as the Westminster Foundation in the United Kingdom.

EXAMPLE – GEORGIA'S PARLIAMENT AND THE DEFENSE BUDGET[59]

USAID supported a program to strengthen parliamentary oversight of the defense budget in Georgia by bringing a former Latin American defense minister to a conference that included representatives of the ministries of defense, finance, and security, as well as NGOs. Themes of the conference were the importance of parliament's role in overseeing the defense budget and the benefits of increased transparency and accountability in the defense budget process. Following the conference, the Ministry of Defense reorganized its budget, submitting line item information to the Parliamentary Defense Committee that enhanced the committee's ability to exercise more effective oversight.

USAID's Experience Strengthening Legislatures,
Washington, D.C.: June 2001, pp. 20-21

---

h. **Military Tasks**

(1) Establish contact and work closely with the AMEMB political section and USAID's democracy and governance officers who are supporting legislative development.

(2) Ensure that agencies supporting legislative strengthening are aware of and plan to support a constructive legislative role in defense and security affairs.

(3) Provide advice and expertise to US civilian agencies, if needed, on the functions and organization of the new legislature to strengthen its role in oversight of the security sector (e.g., formation and role of defense and intelligence committees, defense budget procedures).

(4) Assist with development of infrastructure, facilities, equipment, and material needs of the new legislature, as requested.

(5) Advise local forces on security procedures and arrangements for the new legislature's facilities and members.

i. **Military Planning Considerations**

(1) **The joint force's role in legislative strengthening is likely to focus on logistics and security**. The joint force will support DOS, USAID or international agencies to develop the HN legislature. In order to play a constructive role beyond logistics and security, it will be important to have personnel well grounded in legislative-executive branch mechanisms and procedures for managing defense and security sector issues.

(2) **A parliamentary system is different from a presidential system**. In the presidential system the legislature is separate but equal in theory with the president or head of government. This system is more complex and prone to produce more intense competition for political power. In a post-conflict situation, the executive, especially the

---

military and police, usually has significantly more power than the legislature and may resist efforts to strengthen the legislature at its own expense. It will be especially important for the US military to stress the importance of cooperation with the legislature. It will also be important for the US military to advise international donors on redlines that should not be crossed in strengthening the legislatures role in the defense sector.

**SOME ADDITIONAL PLANNING CONSIDERATIONS
DRAWN FROM UNDP GUIDELINES:**[60]

1.   Recognize the legislative branch's key role in national dialogue processes.

2.   Factor legislature development into designing constitutional and electoral systems.

3.   Ensure timely support to legislatures.

4.   Carefully consider the sequencing and timing of the transition process.

5.   Support constitutional assemblies and/or constitutional committees of the legislature.

6.   Strengthen legislative outreach and legislative forums.

7.   Engage and support sub-national assemblies.

8.   Strengthen the legislative role in reconciliation and transitional justice processes.

9.   Actively support women's and minority groups' political participation.

10.   Support the legislature's efforts to implement commitments to international conventions and gender equality and women's empowerment.

11.   Level the playing field for the opposition.

12.   Foster legislative oversight of the security sector and security related issues as well as oversight of other government departments and agencies.

13.   Involve the legislature in reconstruction processes to insure political buy-in.

14.   Assist the legislature with human rights and rule of law legislation

"Parliaments, Crisis Prevention and Recovery: Guidelines for the International Community, "United Nations Development Programme, 2006, pp. 7-9

---

13. Political Parties

a. Political parties are a central element of democratic systems of governance. They perform essential functions such as: selecting candidates for public office; presenting programs or governing platforms for the voter's consideration; governing with responsibility; in opposition, serving as a "watchdog" that provides a check on the governing party and keeps pressure on it to perform to the best of its ability; acting as a unifying force in government that can overcome regional differences; providing a permanent instrument to assist in the peaceful transfer of power from one group to another; and serving as a humanizing force in government by acting as a buffer between citizens and the complex bureaucracy of modern governments. (Note: This paragraph describes the "ideal type" of political party development and activity. In most developing countries, weak or not, post-conflict or even stable, this is rarely the way parties form and act. This archetype should not be the model [and is not the model] that USG uses in political party development.)

b. As a matter of policy, the US encourages assistance to democratic political parties as one of the building blocks in the construction of a stable nation. USAID is the primary USG agency that implements programs to assist political parties. Working through two key implementing partners, the International Republican Institute (IRI) and the National Democratic Institute for International Affairs (NDI), USAID's focus is on three core areas:

(1) organizational development of political parties;

(2) political parties as linkages between citizens and government; and

(3) strengthening of political parties in government and opposition.[61]

c. The DOS also provides some support for political party development through its Human Rights Democracy Fund (HRDF).

d. In addition to the United States, other countries such as the United Kingdom, Canada, and Australia fund party development programs, usually through non-government organizations (e.g., Australia's Centre for Democratic Institutions). In Europe, there are over thirty foundations, usually affiliated with a political party, that offer party development assistance. The major international organization offering multilateral support to party development is the UNDP. UNDP's work generally falls under three "service lines:" electoral systems and processes; parliamentary development; or policy support for democratic governance. Some UNDP initiatives are directly aimed at political parties (as in Nicaragua and Lesotho), while others involve more indirect support, with parties the secondary beneficiaries (e.g., Zimbabwe and Cambodia).[62] The OSCE's Office for Democratic Institutions and Human Rights also supports party development.[63]

e. Support for political parties, whether bilaterally through US programs or multilaterally through the UN or other international agencies, is a sensitive issue. One concern is whether working to strengthen a party constitutes interference in a sovereign nation's internal affairs. USAID, for example, will not fund programs that are in direct violation of existing domestic laws in a partner country. Another factor to consider is that developing nations often have many small parties operating in a fragmented political system, where weak, unstable governing coalitions may result in frequent elections. Supporting small parties, even though they meet the standards for international support, may work against the goal of stable government. On the other hand, over the long term, strengthening such small parties could result in the eventual growth of an effective political party system.

f. Although political parties are a vital element of a functioning democratic system of government, they can sometimes be based on narrow ethnic, religious or territorial identities or formed around the personality of a party leader. USAID has developed a series of questions to assess whether a political party supports the broader democratic process and is therefore eligible to receive direct or indirect support:

(1) Is the party, both in rhetoric and practice, committed to democratic principles, both organizationally and programmatically?

(2) Does the party leadership engage in elections and use democratic institutions and rules to further its political agenda?

(3) Are party platforms and party leadership chosen and/or validated democratically by party rank-and-file membership?

(4) Has the party and its leadership agreed to respect the outcomes of the electoral process?

(5) If the party (or its leadership) does have a history of violence and anti-democratic behavior, has the current party leadership made credible renunciations of past anti-democratic behavior, backed by actions that demonstrate democratic transformation?

(6) Does the party obey political party, election, and campaign laws?

(7) Does the participation of the party help level the playing field?[64]

g. Electoral influence is another major issue. Section 116(e) of the Foreign Assistance Act authorizes funding for democracy and governance assistance, including support for political parties, but states, "none of these funds may be used, directly or indirectly, to influence the outcome of any election in any country."[65] USAID has identified six areas where it may not provide assistance to political parties:

(1) direct or indirect support for campaigns for public office;

(2) financing of campaigns or candidates for public office;

(3) payments to individuals that are intended to influence their votes;

(4) any direct contribution to a political campaign, or any salary, wage, fee, honoraria, or similar payment to any candidate, political party leader, or campaign official;

(5) funds used for any public meetings that endorse or feature a candidate for public office; and

(6) funds used for any private polls designed to help political campaign strategies in favor of any candidate, party or alliance.[66]

STRENGTHENING POLITICAL PARTIES IN BOSNIA AND HERZEGOVINA[67]

After four years of war, the 1995 Dayton Accord established a political framework to move Bosnia-Herzegovina away from extreme nationalism towards a political system built around democratic institutions and greater political pluralism. Three parties based on Croat, Muslim and Serb nationalism dominated politics in the run-up to the September 1996 elections but an international effort was made to support the development of more moderate multi-ethnic parties that might form an effective opposition. Funded by the National Endowment for Democracy and USAID, the National Democratic Institute for International Affairs (NDI) conducted an intensive political party development program during the run-up to the September elections.

Based on an early assessment mission and requests from key multi-ethnic parties, NDI developed a program that trained multi-ethnic opposition parties on implementing public opinion research; formulating strategic plans; organizing volunteers and events; creating internal communication systems; designing and distributing posters and leaflets; designing radio and TV advertising; promoting effective media relations; and conducting candidate training. The Office of Security Cooperation I Europe (OSCE) also asked NDI to conduct additional training on campaign budgeting and political advertising. To encourage meaningful participation of party representatives in the electoral process, NDI also offered poll-watching training to all registered parties.

Despite the overwhelming advantages of ruling ethnically based parties, opposition parties and independent candidates gained greater access to financing and media coverage. The ratio of ballots case for non-nationalist parties was surprisingly close to pre-war election results, despite the years of ethnic-based warfare. Opposition parties were able to wage campaigns that reached their voters and were able to secure a position in Bosnia and Herzegovina's post-election political system.

Bosnia and Hercegovina (BiH): Strengthening Political Parties, National Democratic Institute for International Affairs (NDI), Washington, D.C.: Spring 1996, pp. 2-5

h.   USAID programming should also conclude or revert to non-campaign activities within 30 days prior to an upcoming election.

THE ROLE OF WOMEN IN INDONESIAN POLITICAL PARTIES[68]

Women are underrepresented as political leaders and elected officials in most regions of the world. Their inclusion in political parties and the electoral process is important to strengthen the democratic, representative nature of political parties and governance. Studies have also shown that countries with higher levels of female participant in government are associated with lower levels of corruption. The National Democratic Institute for International Affairs (NDI) has programs that address women's political participation in a wide range of countries.

In 2000 NDI assisted in the formation of the Women's Political Caucus of Indonesia (KPPI), a multi-party organization of women from all major political parties in Indonesia that has made significant progress in increasing women's involvement in the Indonesian political scene. NDI has worked with KPPI to strengthen its ability to attract new members, develop positions on key topics of importance to women, and train women political leaders. Before the 2004 elections, NDI supported KPPI's efforts to train women candidates and encourage parties to include more women on party election lists. A step in the right direction came with the 2003 law requiring political parties "to consider" selecting women for 30% of the candidates the party puts forward in each electoral district. However, major progress in fully accepting women in leadership roles will require deeper societal and cultural changes in Indonesia.

Assessing Women's Political Party Programs: Best Practices and Recommendations, National Democratic Institute for International Affairs, 2008, p. 3 and p. 46

i. **Military Tasks**

(1) Establish liaison with the AMEMB political officers and USAID democracy and governance officers responsible for political party development.

(2) Assess existing political parties and political leadership and provide assessments to the AMEMB's political section and USAID's democracy and governance officers.

(3) Share information with USG civilian agencies on political leaders who maintain links with militias or paramilitary forces.

(4) Provide information to existing or nascent HN groups seeking US support on US policy in support of democratic political party development. Indicate that USAID, UNDP and other sources of training and support may be available to parties that meet international criteria once security conditions permit.

(5) Provide security, with HN security forces, and support for meetings between various social groups and/or political parties.

(6) Identify needs of US and other programs and determine ways in which military support might supplement their programs (e.g., assistance in printing party materials, media support).

(7) Provide logistic support, such as transportation, for political party poll watchers and monitors when elections are held.

UNDP FOSTERS PARTY DEVELOPMENT IN CAMBODIA[69]

UNDP projects with political parties in Cambodia have been linked to phases of the elections cycle. Working with the newly formed national Election Commission and the Ministry of Information before the 2003 election, UNDP sought to introduce equitable coverage of the parties' election campaigns through support for a program on the main TV and radio stations called "Equity News." The program provided comprehensive coverage of the elections and equitable time to all 23 contesting parties, including the opposition, based on a quota linked to the party's past electoral performance and current popularity. Under the program, parties received advice on how to ensure media coverage, for example by designating media liaison officers and disseminating information about upcoming party events. Equity News was widely considered to be a success, with coverage that included new features such as interviews with party leaders and focus on campaign issues. Since the election, UNDP has continued to work through the Election Commission to support party development in areas such as training party electoral agents on electoral law and procedures, including voter registration. UNDP has also held workshops for parties to promote awareness of Millennium Development Goals (MDG) and encouraged parties to include MDG themes in their campaign platforms.

Assessing Women's Political Party Programs: Best Practices and Recommendations, NDI 2008, p. 62.

---

j. **Military Planning Considerations**

(1) **The joint force's role in political party development is likely to be limited.** In the stabilization tasks matrix developed by the United Kingdom's DFID, for example, there is no military role in party development identified in a non-permissive post-conflict environment and only a civilian role in a permissive environment.[70] However, in an immediate post-conflict situation, the military could find itself working with groups that may evolve into legitimate political parties as the society rebuilds and a more permissive environment permits non-violent and open political competition. Non-state security providers, militias, and other armed groups may seek to transform themselves into legitimate political parties.

(2) **Avoid giving the impression of favoritism in contacts with political party leadership.** In a post-conflict situation, political party leaders may try to use their relationship with military commanders to enhance their party's position. In meeting with party leaders, military commanders should make clear the US position of neutrality between legitimate political parties. Coordination with USAID and the AMEMB Country Team should ensure that a consistent US policy message is delivered.

(3) **The most valuable contribution to political party development will probably be the overall maintenance of security so that parties may engage in peaceful competition.** A fundamental for a functioning political party system is a safe and secure environment that enables them to engage the public and develop constituencies.

---

(4) **There should be no US military footprint on political party development**. All support should be indirect, through existing party development programs such as USAID, NDI, RI, and UNDP.

BASIC PRINCIPLES FROM UNDP[71]

1.   Never allow the US or other international donor name to be used for electoral purposes.

2.   Emphasize indirect or issue-based support in situations that are sensitive or otherwise difficult to call.

3.   Respect the democratic process and always bear in mind that it is the ultimate objective of support.

4.   Work with parties that behave responsibly.

5.   Clearly demarcate the line between capacity development and endorsement.

6.   Refrain from supporting one party in a way that blocks out whole groups of other parties.

7.   Be practical and realistic about US and other international donor internal capacity to interact skillfully with parties.

A Handbook on Working with Political Parties, United Nations Development Programme (UNDP): New York, pp. 41-42

---

14. Civil Society

a. While responsibility for supporting the restoration of civil society falls to civilian USG agencies, IGOs and other international organizations, and NGOs, the JFC may need to take steps to promote civil society if civilian agencies are unable to operate or to operate effectively as a result of a hostile or non-permissive security environment.

b. This section provides the JFC with a basic understanding of the role that joint forces may play in facilitating the restoration of civil society in a country where societal institutions have been degraded or destroyed as a result of conflict or government oppression.

c. The term "civil society" refers to both informal and formal nonstate, not-for-profit organizations and groups that represent the interests of citizens in public discussions. They are one of the primary means of channeling citizens' interests and concerns to the state with the goal of affecting policy and are critical to the effective functioning of a modern democracy. As used in this handbook, "civil society" refers to the broad range of organizations that may express views on government policies, including tribal and ethnic associations, advocacy groups, labor unions, women's organizations, faith-based organizations, professional associations, formal and informal networks, media organizations, social movements, noncommercial business associations, and youth groups. This section does not address the family, organizations representing the state, or commercial enterprises.

d. Like other governance institutions, civil society organizations have an important political role, taking part in establishing policies that balance the interests of the citizens and the state and challenging and debating how things are done and how resources are allocated. Civil society organizations have a critical voice in helping to ensure state accountability and responsiveness, for example by advocating for better public services, serving as a watchdog for improper or inefficient use of public funds, representing citizens' interests in discussions on taxation issues, lobbying legislative bodies regarding the distribution of rights, and campaigning against corruption.

e. Thus far, the influence and impact of returned "expatriates" — country nationals who have been in exile during the conflict — has not been addressed. History shows that these individuals who seek to come back to a post-conflict situation do so with various motives. Some seek to capitalize on their "group" regaining power; others seek to influence politics by collaborating with donors; others seek to reclaim lost economic assets and influence either in government or the private sector. They may bring capital and political power through connections they still retain via kinship or ethnic ties. Iraq and Liberia are two cases in point. Any interaction to support the political processes and CSOs should recognize returned expatriates as a potent source of influence for good or ill. They speak our language and are familiar with our (Western) culture. Finding the helpful ones among them is a challenge.

f. **Military Tasks**

(1) Identify DOS, USAID, IGO, NGO and indigenous civil society initiatives. Military support to civil society will focus on providing security to nurture these initiatives, whenever possible.

(2) In coordination with DOS, USAID, IGOs and other international organizations, and NGOs begin engagement with civil society organizations (CSO) as early as possible, but be careful not to be identified too closely with any one in particular.

(3) Provide logistical support to key civil society leaders to facilitate their participation in public discussions involving the government and citizens.

(4) Encourage HN leaders to engage and seek the views of civil society as new laws and government structures are put into place.

(5) Support civil society efforts to deliver public services and conduct public information campaigns, for example, to promote democracy and tolerance and combat societal violence or discrimination against vulnerable populations.

(6) Provide security to allow DOS, USAID, IGOs and other international organizations, NGOs, and vetted indigenous organizations to conduct technical assistance and training to civil society organizations on subjects related to their operations, including communication skills, transparency, advocacy, tolerance, conflict resolution and capacity building.

h. **Military Planning Considerations**

(1) **Building civil society requires understanding the cultural and historical context of the country.** People in post-conflict and developing societies often have enthusiasm but lack experience in civil society or knowledge of processes to ensure fairness and transparency. Populations formerly dominated by dictatorial regimes may also lack the education and individual skills required to develop democratic institutions and quickly become functioning members of society. Beyond setting up structures and institutions—the skeleton of a democratic government—strengthening civil society requires building individual capacity through training initiatives, long-term mentoring programs, and ultimately increasing institutional capacity.

(2) **Don't Sidetrack Deliberative Public Discussion in Order to Expedite Policy Change**. During the early phases of post-conflict reconstruction, the international community and local political figures may try to expedite political arrangements or rewrite legal frameworks in order to move a particular vision of reform forward without challenge. While expedient, this process discourages citizen participation and reduces the legitimacy of the reform. Like others, some members of civil society have the potential to be spoilers, and it may occasionally be necessary to choose between moving forward on reforms by limiting the parties that are involved in policy discussions. While there are no immutable guidelines for dealing with such situations, it is often more beneficial for the long-term health and stability of the political system to ensure that policy discussions are as inclusive as possible and give an opportunity for all parties to voice their opinions.

(3) **Avoid Inadvertently Encouraging Executive Branch Domination**. While it may be easier and more convenient for advisors to work on legal framework issues through the executive branch directly than to engage civil society and the other branches of government in a dialogue, limiting working contacts to the central government carries the risk of indirectly encouraging the domination of the executive branch and sidestepping civil society in future policy discussions. Persons advising the government on framework issues in the early days of a new administration frequently have the opportunity to influence who is invited to the table to discuss policy. Ensuring civil society representatives are involved within such discussions sets an important precedent for all future policy deliberations by the government.

(4) **Encourage intergroup partnerships and community-building functions at the local level, then linking these efforts to national governance initiatives**. Leveraging local successes by publicizing them at a national level can motivate civil society organization in other parts of the country to come up with their own initiatives, in the process strengthening the acceptance of the sector as a whole.

(5) **Raise the public visibility and status of civil society organizations by including them in public policy discussions and outreach efforts as well as involving them in public service projects conducted by military forces**.

(6) **Include evaluation of the laws governing NGOs and civil society in any assessment of the country's laws and regulations by a competent military or civilian counsel**. The identification of legal restrictions on NGOs and civil society will provide a

basis for USG agencies to work with the HN's executive and legislative branches to amend the law to remove the restrictions.

(7) **Encourage civil society organizations to create or strengthen umbrella organizations that can represent their views to the national government.**

LESSONS LEARNED – THE IMPORTANCE OF CULTURAL SKILLS IN REBUILDING CIVIL SOCIETY IN POST-WAR IRAQ

During the occupation of Iraq, Coalition Provisional Authority (CPA) officials found that Iraqis had been so intimidated by the Saddam regime that individual initiative was almost totally lacking. Because the regime had effectively stamped out civil society, Iraqis did not understand the concept of volunteering for community service. The mushrooming of local government structures, for all of its problems, was one of the success stories of the occupation. Iraqis leaped at the opportunity to be part of new neighborhood, city, district, and provincial councils. Once there, however, they did not know what to do.

Area specialists can be of great assistance by designing structures that are likely to be accepted by local populations and easily integrated into the existing culture. They are also critical in the execution stage, particularly those with language skills. Additionally, attempts should be made to break certain local habits. For example, when Iraqis completed job applications, they often provided their ethnic background and religious sect, an undemocratic practice the CPA wished to discourage. Taking local practices and culture into account can smooth the transition toward democracy.

Multiple sources, to include *Special Inspector General for Iraq Reconstruction (SIGIR), Hard Lessons: The Iraq Reconstruction Experience.* Washington, DC: US Government Printing Office, 2009

---

15. Special Governance Topics

a. Political Reconciliation

(1) Political reconciliation[72] involves establishing relationships and building political and social order in countries where they have never existed, or have been damaged or destroyed through conflict. Reconciliation is an essential element and outcome in resolving conflict and achieving an enduring peace that allows international military forces to disengage from a region. JFCs can make a critical contribution to political reconciliation by creating an environment that is conducive to dialogue between parties to the conflict.

(2) The JFC will support political reconciliation primarily through provision of security to DOS, USAID, UN and other sanctioned IGOs, and NGOs. When joint forces must directly participate in political reconciliation, they should transfer reconciliation efforts to civilian USG, international, or indigenous leaders as soon as possible.

(3) The methods to promote reconciliation will vary by country and culture. It is not possible to design a single template for conducting a successful political reconciliation effort or for US joint forces support to such an effort. The following considerations should inform operational design:

(a) Should reconciliation be pursued on the basis of groups or individuals?

(b) Successful reconciliation of leading insurgents may require HN leaders to act as patrons and guarantee defecting insurgents protection some degree of authority and status after switching sides.

(c) Reconciliation strategies based on individuals withdrawing from the conflict need to be supported by efforts to protect such individuals from retaliation and provide them with opportunities for employment and reintegration into society.

RECONCILIATION EXAMPLE: THE "SONS OF IRAQ"

In Iraq, US forces countered the Sunni-based insurgency by hiring "Sons of Iraq," a group that included former insurgents, to provide security in Sunni-dominated provinces. By mid-2008, there were roughly 90,000 "Sons," who were paid $300 a month. The program was related to and facilitated by the "awakening" movement involving the formation of coalitions of tribal sheikhs beginning in 2005 to provide security against terrorist and sectarian violence.

Special Inspector General for Iraq Reconstruction (SIGIR), *Hard Lessons: The Iraq Reconstruction Experience.* Washington, DC: US Government Printing Office, 2009, page 297

---

(4) Building trust and communication between groups are important elements of reconciliation. However, to achieve enduring solutions, reconciliation must address the distribution of the power within the HN government, while simultaneously as addressing the desire of aggrieved parties for justice and an accurate account of past abuses and injustices for the historical record. Parties may be willing to compromise with assurances that each side will have a role in governance. In such a compromise, power is shared on a permanent basis by the major segments of society. The basic forms that a power-sharing arrangement may take include: a coalition government in which leaders of the major political parties have positions; arrangements that provide special benefits and protections for minority groups; systems in which power is decentralized and distributed among autonomous sub-national units, and agreements that require major government decisions to be made by consensus.

b. **Military Planning Considerations**. The joint force will generally conduct the following activities in support of and in coordination with the DOS and USAID. Their preparation is also an appropriate consideration in operational design, ideally in the ICAF.

(1) **Promote political dialogue**. JFCs can promote reconciliation by sponsoring and supporting political dialogue between representatives of opposing groups and communities.

(2) **Promote increased intercommunal contacts**. In situations where there are deep communal divisions in the HN, commandeers should work to create opportunities for intergroup collaborative projects that can be employed to promote reconciliation at a local level.

(3) **Concentrate on building a new political and moral order and social relationships rather than restoring the preconflict order**. In many cases – for example, in the internal conflicts in Peru, Guatemala, and South Africa in the latter half of the 20th century – reconciliation meant building relationships between social and ethnic groups that did not exist prior to the conflict.

(4) **Avoid exacerbating intergroup tensions by understanding the local political and social landscape**. Military planners and commanders should be aware of possible social and political dimensions of interactions between US armed forces and the local population to avoid unintentionally exacerbating intergroup tensions or rivalries. For example, in an impoverished region, the wages paid to locally-hired support personnel may be one of the only sources of cash income in the area. If such jobs are allowed to be monopolized by members of one group or clan, it could add to resentment in other segments of the population.

(5) **Balance prosecution for crimes against the need to maintain stability**. A dilemma in some post-conflict environments is the tension between satisfying the oppressed segment of the population's sense of justice against foregoing or delaying prosecution of past abuses to maintain social and political stability. In many cases, leaders of previously discredited regimes may retain strong support in the population, as well as in the military and other security forces. Prosecuting them carries the risk of igniting widespread violence or a return to conflict. On the other hand, allowing leaders and elites associated with past abuses to play a role in the government can short circuit reconciliation and undercut HN legitimacy. In Africa, there is a recent tradition of "Truth and Reconciliation" processes that allow those guilty of abuses or crimes to come into the open. An example of this is Rwandan National Unity and Reconciliation Commission and the establishment of traditional forms of accountability, such as gacaca courts. Details available at http://www.nurc.gov.rw/ and http://www.justiceinperspective.org.za/ index.php?option=comcontent&task=view&id=27&Itemid=59. This process has tended to expedite healing and resolution of past grievances.

c. Anti-Corruption

(1) Corruption is often defined as "the abuse of entrusted authority for private gain."[73] It is a major political and economic problem in most post-conflict situations, undermining the legitimacy of government, draining essential resources from the state, and increasing the risk of instability and return to conflict. There are several types of corruption, including petty individual corruption (e.g., minor bribes), bureaucratic corruption (e.g., contracting kickbacks), criminal corruption (e.g., criminal gangs extorting regular pay-offs from legitimate businesses),

and political corruption (e.g., manipulating criminal investigations, carrying out or covering up political killings).

"Throughout the US reconstruction program, Iraqi corruption 'exerted a corrosive force upon [the] fledgling democracy,' contributing to a flight of capital that 'directly harmed the country's economic viability." [74]

"Corruption is like terrorism, even more dangerous than terrorism. It disintegrates the country and affects everything." [75]

Mohmoud Othman, independent member of Parliament, Iraq. Quoted in The Washington Post, May 10, 2009

(2) There are two general approaches to fighting corruption: prevention focuses on corruption as a symptom of poor governance, while enforcement emphasizes criminal or administrative punishments as well as strengthening investigation and prosecution.

(3) Developing the capacity of the HN to address corruption is critical to good governance. Corruption can pose a serious threat to reconstruction and stabilization efforts. It can undercut the construction and maintenance of infrastructure, deprive people of goods and services, reduce confidence in public institutions, and potentially aid insurgent groups reportedly funded by graft derived from smuggling or embezzlement.[76]

(4) The HN and third country militaries can be vulnerable to corruption because the defense sector in many countries operates with a great deal of secrecy, which can be used to avoid oversight and veil corruption. Abuses of power in the defense sector affect other sectors as well; every dollar lost to corruption is a dollar not spent for other needs. A 2006 survey indicated that roughly one third of international defense companies felt that they recently had lost out on a contract because of corruption by a competitor. The role of weak accountability in procurement is often associated with corruption in defense. It is difficult for outside entities to oversee large, infrequent, and technically complex contracts. Large sums of money, a lack of transparency and accountability, and the temptation to profit from procurement contribute to potential corruption of the process.

(5) There are three broad sources of corruption in the defense sector:

(a) **Defense Officials (Ministerial and Military Staff)**. Failure to observe agreed standards of business conduct, bribery of public officials to bend military rules, cash payoffs to pass security and other checkpoints.

(b) **Defense Institutions (Ministries and Armed Forces)**. Profiteering from procurement, profiteering from soldiers' payroll, income from state-owned assets, self-serving use of budgets and resources, receiving benefits from private defense companies, misuse of reward, promotion and disciplinary processes.

(c) **Political Influence**. Non-agreed defense policy, underestimated or off-budget defense spending, dishonest leadership and secret power networks, involvement in elections and politics and misuse of power to influence legislation and parliamentary investigations, corrupt judicial processes, organized crime links, control of intelligence and misuse of related powers, state capture and the de facto, illicit takeover of defense.[77]

(6) A post-conflict setting poses special challenges for anti-corruption efforts:

(a) **Weak Political Commitment**. Assistance programs will not be optimally effective unless local political leaders are committed to combating corruption. Corruption can facilitate spoilers' access to resources that can then be used to fund insurgencies or undermine government institutions.

(b) **Capacity**. Limited capacity, even when senior leadership is strongly committed, creates challenges for effective anti-corruption policies.

(c) **Social Conditions not Conducive for Change**. Insecurity, fractionalization, and the breakdown of social norms and rule of law make it difficult for people to stand up against corruption or avoid taking part in illicit activities.

(d) **Unfavorable Economic Conditions**. Often black markets and illicit trade thrive in the chaotic process of rebuilding an economy.

(e) **Absorptive Capacity**. The massive influx of resources during post-conflict reconstruction can be a catalyst for corruption.

(7) Ideally, a successful fight against corruption requires that three important factors be present:

(a) In the post-conflict phase, the end of fighting and establishment of relative security, in particular when fighting has ended in stalemate.

(b) Political will to combat corruption.

(c) Public investment in the fight against corruption (a public that makes clear to leadership that corruption is unacceptable and that has the means to make its views known enforceable).

(8) If these prerequisites are met, the HN's best chance of limiting corruption is through seeking to build:

(a) a trustworthy and effective criminal justice system with an independent judicial branch, an independent and adequately resourced prosecutorial authority, and an independent and adequately resourced defense bar;

(b) a transparent and accountable political process;

(c) a stronger and more capable public administration, with barriers to cronyism and nepotism;

(d) government accountability to public opinion (via responsible, free media and open elections);

(e) a sustainable and legitimate government revenue stream; and

(f) effective government regulation and stimulation of an open market economy.

Many US government agencies, including the US Agency for International Development (USAID), the Department of the Treasury, and the Department of Justice are involved in combating corruption. On the ground, USAID is often the key US government agency working on corruption issues and may be able to provide information on international organizations and NGOs involved in anti-corruption programs.

VARIOUS SOURCES

---

d. **Military Planning Considerations**. The joint force will generally conduct the following activities in support of and in coordination with the DOS and USAID. Their preparation is also an appropriate consideration in operational design, ideally in the ICAF.

(1) **The role of military forces in anti-corruption efforts will vary depending on conditions within the operational environment**. In a non-permissive, i.e., uncertain or hostile, environment, the military may lead reform efforts. Even when nonmilitary agencies are present, the security situation may still require extensive military support to civilian efforts. Once the security situation permits normal civilian activity, the military role is usually limited to the HN defense sector.

**LESSONS LEARNED: CORRUPTION AND
THE IRAQ RECONSTRUCTION EXPERIENCE[78]**

1. Corruption can thrive in an environment of post-conflict reconstruction because large-scale reconstruction programs combine "large public procurement projects, major funding infusions, and inadequate government economic management." Corruption was pervasive in Iraq and fundamentally impeded US efforts to develop ministry capacity.

2. To be effective, anti-corruption programs should be well coordinated and well funded. US efforts to develop effective Iraqi anticorruption oversight institutions produced mixed results because of underfunding and lack of coordination among the USG agencies managing programs.

---

3. Local institutional capacity and cultural context must be considered when developing anti-corruption programs. Inspectors General appointed by the CPA and placed in each ministry were viewed by many Iraqis as foreign entities inserted into Iraq's body politic by the Americans, and many considered them to be spies for the Americans.

SIGIR, *Hard Lessons: The Iraq Reconstruction Experience.* Washington, DC: US Government Printing Office, 2009, pages 206-16

(2) **The pressure and chaos of an emergency can result in neglecting recordkeeping and competitive procurement rules.** In the longer term, these same problems can occur if weak government institutions are overwhelmed with assistance. It is important to be aware of absorptive capacity.

(3) **Areas for anti-corruption training include prevention of military procurement fraud and professional audit and control standards (including the defense budget).**

(4) **If the HN is party to international treaties and conventions on anti-corruption, advisors may be able to use this to justify stronger anti-corruption efforts within the armed forces and defense/security ministries.** Relevant international treaties and conventions include: the OECD DAC Governance Network-Collective Action Against Corruption; the OECD Convention on Combating Bribery of Foreign Public Officials in International Business Transactions (OECD Anti-Bribery Convention); the UN Convention Against Corruption; the UN Convention Against Transnational Organized Crime (UNTOC); and the Stolen Assets Recovery Initiative (StAR).

(5) **Avoid raising unrealistic expectations.** Overly ambitious anti-corruption promises that cannot be implemented risk undermining the credibility and legitimacy of international donors and local leaders.

(6) **Checks and balances are critical elements in preventing corruption, even though they may slow down rebuilding efforts.** Checks and balances should include legislative oversight of budgets and strengthening the role of the judiciary to ensure accountability.

(7) **The long-term costs of including corrupt elites as part of a post-conflict government needs to be balanced against the need for post-conflict stability.** If it is impossible to exclude corrupt leaders from government, establishing a transitional government for a specific time may help.

q. **Anti-corruption initiatives should fall under a comprehensive, coordinated rule of law program.** The lack of any concentrated responsibility for rule of law reform meant that there was no coordinated leadership on rule of law initiatives and a paucity of personnel devoted to the effort. A DOS review of the rule of law in Iraq found that there was an absence of coordination and that the USG had been very slow to disburse the few funds allocated for rule-of-law projects, particularly regarding capacity building.

16. Security Force Assistance, Security Sector Reform, and Governance

"...arguably, the most important military component in the War on Terror is not the fighting we do ourselves, but how well we enable and empower our partners to defend and govern their own countries."

Secretary of Defense Robert Gates, 2007

a. Security Force Assistance (SFA) is an integral component of Security Assistance (SA)[79] and Security Sector Reform (SSR).[80] SSR, in turn, is fundamentally linked to good governance, and therefore is an important task for US military planners to consider in reconstruction and stabilization missions. See the *Rule of Law and Security Sector Reform Handbook* for a more comprehensive treatment of these important concepts and practices.

b. **Security Force Assistance**

(1) Security force assistance, which is a subset of security cooperation and foreign internal defense (FID),[81] covers the entire spectrum of the security sector, "from the ministerial level to the patrolling police officer and soldier."[82] Through SFA, commanders work with the ministries responsible for national and internal security, including the ministry of national defense, the interior ministry, and the justice ministry.[83] SFA commanders work to assess strengths and weaknesses of the relevant ministries and the training requirements of their employees.[84]

(2) Security force assistance has received increased attention in recent years, culminating in the publication of the US Army's FM 3-07.1, *Security Force Assistance* (May 2009), as well as the revision of JP 3-07.1, *Foreign Internal Defense*. FM 3-07.1 and JP 3-07.1 address The United States' inability to enable our partners to strengthen their defense sector, and thus become less reliant on US support. Special operations forces traditionally tasked to train HN forces did not have the capacity to carry out the greatly expanded SFA initiative envisioned by the Secretary of Defense.[85]

SECURITY FORCE ASSISTANCE

"Security force assistance **is the unified action to generate, employ, and sustain local, host-nation or regional security forces in support of a legitimate authority."**[86] **SFA improves the capability and capacity of host-nation or regional security organization's security forces. These include not only military forces, but also police, paramilitary, and intelligence forces; border police, coast guard, and customs officials; and prison guards and correctional personnel at all levels of government within a nation state, as well as other local and regional forces.**[87]

FM 3-07.1, p. 1-1; Joint Center for International Security Force Assistance (JCISFA), *Commander's Handbook for Security Force Assistance,* **p. 1**

---

b. **Security Sector Reform**

(1) Security sector reform, as a discipline, is emerging in recognition of the changing security environment and the limitations of existing USG interagency, UN and international organization, and donor approaches. Through SSR, the USG seeks to work in partnership with other governments and organizations to support peace, security, and democratic governance globally.[88] Support to SSR involves a number of US civilian agencies, especially the USAID, as well as a range of bilateral donors and international organizations.

(2) SSR is the set of policies, plans, programs, and activities that a government undertakes to improve the way it provides safety, security, and justice. The overall objective is to provide these services in a way that promotes an effective and legitimate public service that is transparent, accountable to civilian authority, and responsive to the needs of the public. From a donor perspective, SSR is an umbrella term that might include integrated activities in support of: defense and armed forces reform; civilian management and oversight; justice; police; corrections; intelligence reform; national security planning and strategy support; border management; disarmament, demobilization, and reintegration (DDR); and reduction of armed violence.[89]

(3) Improving governance within the security sector is an important component of security sector reform. For SSR to succeed, security institutions should be accountable and transparent. **Security sector governance** is the transparent, accountable, and legitimate management and oversight of security policy and practice. Fundamental to all SSR engagement is the recognition that good governance – effective, equitable, responsive, transparent, and accountable management of public affairs and resources – and the rule of law are essential to an effective security sector. Democratic and effective security sector governance expands the concept of civilian "control" to include administration, management, fiscal responsibility, policy formulation, and service delivery.[90]

SSR PROGRAM IN LIBERIA[91]

The US is carrying out perhaps its most complex SSR effort in Liberia, where the Accra Comprehensive Peace Agreement (CPA), signed in August 2003, ended fourteen years of conflict. In 2004, the Department of State began a project with the Liberian Government to demobilize and rebuild the Armed Forces of Liberia and the Ministry of Defense. (The UN Mission in Liberia is implementing police reform.) To date the program, which was contracted out to private security companies, has demobilized nearly 14,000 soldiers. The program is designed to create a new force structure and table of organization, to replace arms and equipment and to refurbish military bases. The goal is a professional army of 2,000 personnel, modeled on US military doctrine and supporting the national objectives of the Government of Liberia by September 2010. The US-Liberia SSR program, supported by the UN and other bilateral donors, is not without controversy. The use of private contractors has been questioned by some, while others have noted that the program, with its focus on training and equipping the armed forces and police, has neglected to take a comprehensive approach to include areas such as military and criminal justice reform.[92] **After an evaluation visit to Liberia in September 2007, a US interagency team made a series of recommendations that, when implemented, should strengthen a comprehensive approach to the SSR effort.**

Sean McFate, *Securing the Future: A Primer on Security Sector Reform in Conflict Countries*, United States Institute of Peace Special Report 209, September 2008, pp. 15-16.

c. Security Force Assistance, Security Sector Reform, and Governance

(1) Security force assistance, security sector reform, and governance are closely linked. SFA seeks to develop security forces that contribute to the legitimate governance of the local populace, including moral and political legitimacy of the HN government. Each SFA mission ultimately aims to support the relationship between the local government and the people.[93] Through SFA, commanders are asked to establish and maintain the rule of law and to eliminate corruption, torture, excessive use of force, improper detention, and graft.[94]

(2) SSR is a multidisciplinary effort that includes activities in support of security force and intelligence reform; justice sector reform; civilian oversight and management; community security; and disarmament, demobilization and reintegration (DDR) programs. There is an important relationship between development agencies working to establish stable institutional structures and governance frameworks and the military that works with the security sector. Often this relationship is recognized too late, resulting in imbalances that can undermine the whole stabilization and reconstruction effort. Governance can be seriously undermined if, for example, security forces grow without regard to the overall fiscal and economic environment; police forces are developed without attention to other parts of the justice system (e.g., courts, prisons); or there is creation of forces without proper oversight and accountability systems in place. Moreover, funding and other assistance provided to ministries of defense and interior without similar strengthening of other ministries can result in defense and interior dominating the other weaker ministries in a post-conflict government.

(3) Attempts to reform the security sector are highly political, often threatening the power base of important elites within society, and can in fact be dangerous, especially in countries where the security sector has been the strongest pre-conflict institution. Losers in the reform process often have the influence and resources to sabotage the process. Reform can sometimes trigger reprisals and may even spark a renewed outbreak of violent conflict.

(4) SSR can influence governance in several ways, including through elections assistance. If an election is being held during a post-conflict period, for example, US personnel may be required to help train local forces to provide security and support for the election process while remaining neutral and refraining from intervening.

(5) Long-term development demands a sufficient degree of security to facilitate poverty reduction and economic growth. Physical insecurity is a central concern of poor

populations around the world; security forces that are untrained, ill-equipped, mismanaged and irregularly paid are often part of the problem, and perpetrate serious violations of human rights. Effective and accountable security institutions are therefore essential for sustainable peace and development. Security sector reform underscores that effectiveness, accountability and democratic governance are mutually reinforcing elements of security.[95]

d. Joint Planning Considerations

(1) **SSR objectives are developed within the context of strategic guidance during operational design.**[96] As contingency operations develop, the JFC will develop more specific SSR objectives with DOS regional and country teams, USAID regional experts and possibly UN and international organization personnel, as well as allied and coalition partners. "Post conflict" transition, however, will be the best forum to develop specific SSR tasks.[97]

(2) **Provision of security must be balanced with building capacity for rule of law, justice, and democratic governance.** Excessive focus on security without concurrent governance development will make sequential development of SSR objectives impossible. Sequencing is further complicated when international assistance programs move forward before the HN government has identified its priorities.[98]

COMPONENTS OF THE SECURITY SYSTEM

1. **Core Security Agencies** — police, gendarmeries, paramilitaries, presidential guards, intelligence and security services (military and civilian), coast guards, border guards, customs authorities, and reserve or local security units (civil defense, national guards, militias

2. **Management and Oversight Bodies** — the executive, national security advisory bodies, legislative committees, ministries of defense, internal affairs, foreign affairs, customary and traditional authorities, financial management bodies, and civil society organizations

3. **Justice and Rule Of Law** — judiciary and justice ministries; prisons; criminal investigation and prosecution services' human rights commissions and ombudsmen; and customary and traditional justice systems

VARIOUS SOURCES

---

(3) **Short-term force generation requirements should be balanced against adherence to longer-term SSR principles to avoid creating an overly militarized society.** In a post-conflict environment, security is an immediate concern and rapidly building security forces, both military and police, is a top priority. Building security without developing governance and rule of law, however, can undercut operational objectives and work against the strategic interest of the United States by perpetuating local conflicts and instability.

(4) **Legislative and judicial oversight of the security sector is a consistent long-term USG objective**. Appropriate checks and balances can help prevent the executive from dominating through built-in institutional advantage. Accountability and oversight mechanisms outside of the executive can help prevent abuses of power and corruption and build public confidence.

(5) **Reconstituted security forces, especially the national army, should be firmly under the control and management of the newly established civilian government**. Agreements that split management or oversight between rivals are unsustainable and may lead to more violence. Use of traditional or tribal militias at the local level may provide short-term stability but lead to longer-term problems if local militias refuse to disarm or to integrate their forces with government security forces. Moreover, local tribal or militia leaders who have been empowered during a conflict may use their expanded power base to challenge the authority of the new, post-conflict government.

(6) **The Ministry of Interior (or a similar bureaucratic agency responsible for the police and other internal security forces) must be also be reformed to sustain tactical reforms**. Often international donors go straight to training the police, with little attention to the interior ministry to which the police report.[99]

(7) **It is difficult to find qualified civilian leaders and staff to manage and oversee the security sector in many post-conflict countries**. Appointment of local power brokers may help keep the peace and reduce crime, but can also undermine the legitimacy of new security institutions.

(8) **Advisors in security ministries should not merely be experts but should be negotiators, teachers and partners**. They must be able to establish a meaningful dialogue with local leaders in order to provide useful, substantive advice. Patience and humility are important traits. The characteristics of successful advisors differ from those required to actually execute the task for which they are advising, particularly in the military context. Successful military commanders may not be successful advisors.[100]

(9) **Delivering justice, while at the same time preserving stability in a society coming out of conflict, requires maintaining a delicate balance**.

(10) **Non-statutory security forces** — liberation armies, guerrilla armies, private security companies, political party militias[101]

17. Ungoverned Areas and Safe Havens

a. Following 9/11, national security specialists began to focus on potential threats that could originate in areas of the world where central government authority was very weak or non-existent, an issue identified the 9/11 Commission. The Ungoverned Areas Project, under the management of the Under Secretary of Defense for Policy, produced a final report in early 2008 after a series of interagency workshops, consultations with USG experts and a review of scholarly research.[102]

"To find sanctuary, terrorist organizations have fled to some of the least governed, most lawless places in the world. The intelligence community has prepared a world map that highlights possible terrorist havens . . . areas that combine rugged terrain, weak governance, room to hide or receive supplies, and low population density with a town or city near enough to allow necessary interaction with the outside world. Large areas scattered around the world meet these criteria."[103]

9/11 Commission On Ungoverned Areas

b. In a review of the strategic environment, the US *National Defense Strategy* (June 2008) also identifies "ungoverned, under-governed, misgoverned and contested areas" as "fertile ground" for insurgent groups and other non-state organizations "to exploit gaps in governance capacity of local regimes to undermine local stability and regional security."[104]

c. The RAND Corporation has conducted extensive research into the problem of ungoverned areas and published a study in 2007 that included eight case studies (the Pakistani-Afghan border, the Arabian Peninsula, the Sulawesi-Mindanao arc, the East African corridor from Sudan southwards, West Africa from Nigeria westward, the North Caucasus, the Columbian-Venezuelan border, and the Guatemala-Chiapas border).[105]

WHAT ARE UNGOVERNED AREAS AND SAFE HAVENS?[106]

Ungoverned Area – A place where the state or the central government is unable or unwilling to extend control, effectively govern, or influence the local population, and where a provincial, local, tribal, or autonomous government does not fully or effectively govern, due to inadequate governance capacity, insufficient political will, gaps in legitimacy, the presence of conflict, or restrictive norms of behavior.

Safe Haven – a place or situation that enables illicit actors to operate while evading detection or capture, including ungoverned, under-governed, misgoverned, or contest physical area (remote, urban maritime) or exploitable non-physical areas (virtual) where illicit actors can organize, plan, raise funds, communicate, recruit, train, and operate in relative security.

Robert D. Lamb, Final Report of the Ungoverned Areas Project, prepared for the Office of the Under Secretary of Defense for Policy

d. **A Framework for Ungoverned Areas/Safe Havens.** In its study of the ungoverned area/safe havens (UGA/SH) problem, the Office of the Deputy Assistant Secretary of Defense for Policy Planning, in collaboration with other USG agencies, developed a framework to facilitate collaboration among offices and units that address UGA/SH problems. Agencies in defense, diplomacy, development, and law enforcement all have capabilities to counter the threats of UGA/SH. The framework can be used to systematically account for geographical, political, civil, and resource factors that make safe havens possible. The considerations identified in the framework can be used to build relevant strategies, capabilities and doctrines, best practices, or to facilitate collaboration among USG components that address UGA/SH problems – whether openly, discreetly, or covertly – to ensure unity of effort. The core of the framework consists of two sections:

(1) What makes safe havens possible? (Geographic, political, civil, and resource considerations)

(2) What makes a safe haven problematic to US security? (Foreign policy, military operations, weapons of mass destruction, the presence of transnational illicit organizations with projection capabilities or partnerships that act as force multipliers, natural resources, public opinion, foreign influence, proximity to the US homeland, and the susceptibility of the problem to US action)

AN APPROACH TO WORKING IN UNGOVERNED AREAS[107]

Under the Cross Border Conflict Mitigation Initiative, the US Agency for International Development (USAID) supports coalitions of state and non-state actors to perform governance functions in ungoverned areas. In the pastoralist arc of the Horn of Africa, governance coalitions consisting of women, religious and traditional leaders and community activists in border areas build relationships and negotiate agreements on issues such as grazing, migration and watering arrangements as well as agreements to stop hostilities. USAID support is in the form of direct grants to NGOs and specialized technical assistance and training to groups involved in project development, conflict management and peace building.

USAID, *Building Peace along Borders in East Africa*

---

e. **Unity of effort is important, but no single approach exists**. Not all ungoverned areas present a threat to the US, however the military planner will find that ungoverned or weakly governed areas are often the focus of military operations. There is no USG-wide doctrine to address ungoverned areas and safe havens. Multiple agencies and programs may address the problems from various approaches (e.g., counterinsurgency (COIN), counternarcotics, counterterrorism, development assistance, etc.). Programs to extend effective governance should be a key component of any civilian programs, and joint planners must ensure their efforts are coordinated with the DOS, USAID and other civilian agencies, pursuant to USG policy. In the words of the *National Defense Strategy*, addressing the problem of ungoverned areas "will require local partnerships and creative approaches to deny extremists the opportunity to gain footholds."[108]

18. Governance and Counterinsurgency

a. Governance and COIN are intimately linked. Insurgencies thrive in an environment of weak, inefficient, and corrupt governance. The inability of a government to address grievances, whether they are real or perceived, provides fuel for an insurgent movement.

COUNTERINSURGENCY – IMPROVING GOVERNANCE[109]

"Almost by definition, a government facing insurgency will require a degree of political 'behavior modification' (substantive political reform, anti-corruption and governance improvement) in order to successfully address the grievances that gave rise to insurgency in the first place. Supporting nations may be able to assist in these reforms."

US Government Counterinsurgency Guide, January 2009, p. 24

b. Insurgencies and efforts to counter them are not new and there is a large body of literature on the subject. The wars in Afghanistan and Iraq have resulted in renewed focus on counterinsurgency and the production of two key guides for US military planners: 1) the US Army's FM 3-24, *Counterinsurgency*,[110] and 2) the *US Government Counterinsurgency Guide*, produced jointly by the DOS, DOD, and the USAID.

c. The two documents both stress the importance of the United States taking a whole-of-government approach. Both also recognize that strengthening governance in the affected country as an essential element in counterinsurgency.

KEY DEFINITIONS

Insurgency – the organized use of subversion and violence to seize, nullify, or challenge political control of a region.

Counterinsurgency – the comprehensive civilian and military efforts taken to simultaneously defeat and contain insurgency and address its root causes.[111]

US Government Counterinsurgency Guide, January 2009

d. **Approaches**. There are two basic approaches to COIN: enemy-centric and population-centric. Enemy-centric campaigns may be effective when an insurgency is led or centrally controlled by a charismatic or powerful person. However, a population-centric approach has historically proven more successful against most insurgencies. In this approach, efforts are concentrated on gaining the support of the population by improving "the quality of governance through political reform, strengthening the rule of law and conducing economic development."[112] At the same time, the insurgents must be contained or weakened through a combination of diplomacy, negotiation, police, intelligence, and military efforts and operations.

e. **Elements of a COIN Strategy**. The *US Government Counterinsurgency Guide* uses a COIN model consisting of five components:[113]

(1) **Political** – All COIN activities are organized around this key strategic intervention involving political reconciliation and reform of governance. Political strategy in COIN "focuses on strengthening the government's capability and capacity to respond – and be seen to be responding – to the needs of its people."

(2) **Economic** – the provision of essential services and long-term economic growth, with the aim of generating confidence in the government and reducing frustrated, unemployed youth, a potential source of insurgent recruits.

(3) **Security** – the enabler for the other functions which involves developing the affected state's entire security sector, not just its military force.

(4) **Information** – comprises intelligence and influence to promote the affected government's cause.

(5) **Control** – the end result is that the affected government controls its territory with the support of the population.

f. The US Army's FM 3-24 provides an example of a slightly different approach, with five LOOs, all supported by information operations that have an end state of increased support from the populace for the government. The LOOs are: combat operations/civil security operations; HN security forces; essential services; economic development; and governance.[114]

CIVILIAN-MILITARY ROLES – FACING REALITY[115]

"Where the security environment prevents US civilian agencies from operating freely, the US military may be required to provide extensive support to political, economic and governance efforts in their stead. This will be the case during the 'establishment of control' phase in every COIN campaign and, in many cases, throughout the campaign. Given the difference in risk acceptance and the large and enduring resource imbalance between civilian and military agencies this is simply a fact of life: officials and policy maker must plan for it accordingly."

FM 3-24, *Counterinsurgency*, p. 5-3

g. **What is success?**

(1) It is often difficult to determine when COIN has succeeded, "but improved governance will usually bring about marginalization of the insurgents to the point at which they are destroyed, co-opted or reduced to irrelevance in numbers and capability."[116]

(2) It is also important, however, to understand how a robust COIN effort can affect (e.g., detract from) other programs supporting governance reform. How the two co-exist in the same strategic framework is a product of both program design and strategic communication. Misunderstandings that spring from friction between the two objectives can undermine both and create confusion about true USG motives. A robust joint civilian-military planning and coordination effort is essential in country situations where COIN and Governance programs are high priority.

19. Summary of Military Tasks and Planning Considerations

A matrix of the military tasks and planning considerations developed above may be found in Appendix A.

Intentionally Blank

CHAPTER III
MILITARY SUPPORT TO POST-CONFLICT ELECTIONS

"No major security incidents occurred during the Afghan presidential elections on 9 October 2004. This achievement was the result of intensified and coordinated efforts by the government and the international community to strengthen national police and armed forces. It also depended heavily on the contribution of the 18,000-strong multinational forces of the US-led Coalition present in Afghanistan."[117]

United Nations Peacekeeping Best Practices Unit

1. Introduction and Military Problem

a. In a post-conflict environment, elections are often one of the first and most visible steps toward democratic political transition, signaling the transfer of authority from the international community to HN leaders. In this context, the ability of US or coalition forces to conduct an election support mission successfully, in particular through achieving a secure environment, can be critical to the establishment of a legitimate democratic government and attainment of overall mission objectives. Without the establishment of a secure environment, an election is prone to failure. Rather than promoting the government's credibility and the capabilities of indigenous security forces, extensive violence during an election can highlight the government and security force ineffectiveness.

b. While consideration must be given to the timing of the elections to ensure that they are not conducted before the government and HN security forces are prepared, it does not necessarily follow that all threats must be defeated prior to holding an election. During the first decade of this century, elections in both Iraq and Afghanistan have demonstrated that voting can be conducted despite threats posed by insurgents or discontented political parties, provided that there is close planning and synchronization of security efforts between US and coalition forces, HN security forces and election officials, IGOs and other international organizations, and civilian agencies and stakeholders involved in the election process.

THE MILITARY PROBLEM

How can the joint force commander support a host-nation led election process in a manner that underscores the sovereignty and independence of the HN and culminates in the peaceful transfer of power and formation of a legitimate government?

---

c. This chapter assists JFCs prepare to support a post-conflict election. It presents an operational framework for joint force activities that captures the entire election process, outlining key military tasks and planning considerations as well as key partner agencies and stakeholders that have a role in an election process. The key to the success is for military planners to understand that an election is more than a single-day event, but rather a multistage process that requires comprehensive planning and involves discrete tasks in the various stages of the election process.

2. Strategic Election Planning, Programming, and Budgeting

a. As outlined in the State Department guide, Transition Elections and Political Processes in Reconstruction and Stabilization Operations: Lessons Learned,[118] the strategic planning process for post-conflict elections and related political processes should involve at least five steps that are outlined in detail below. While planning for election operations ideally would take place on an interagency basis, joint force planners should anticipate leading the planning process if security and logistics are dominant concerns and HN forces are not yet capable of executing tasks related to those concerns on their own.

b. In planning election operations, civilian and military planners must assess the country context, the main obstacles or problems likely to be encountered, and the political, legal, and funding context for interventions (both USG and international). The plan should be built around a common USG goal for the election process and identify a combination of activities connected to this goal. It must identify a budget. Finally, it must identify interconnections between elections, political parties, and other post-conflict activities.

c. From a joint force perspective, planners should anticipate that military forces may be integrally involved in all phases of the election process usually in a supporting role to USG and HN civilian leadership. However, as demonstrated by the active role of military forces in supporting elections in Bosnia, Afghanistan, and Iraq, joint forces need to be prepared to execute an extensive number of tasks in connection with elections in a post-conflict environment as conditions demand.

d. In general, the assessment process follows this approximate sequence:

(1) **Step 1: Assess conditions on ground, the main obstacles or problems that may be encountered, and USG political, legal, and funding context.**

(a) An assessment is essential to ground the plan in a comprehensive understanding of the problems that must be addressed for the election to succeed. To do this, it is important to understand:

1. the context of the prior conflict and how it will influence the environment in which the elections will take place;

2. what effect the political and electoral process will have on that context;

3. whether there is an agreement on rules governing the election and structures of the new government;

4. those who have a stake in the outcome (see text box on election participants);

5. stakeholders' interests, sources of legitimacy, and resources; and

6. potential scenarios.

(b) Once this analysis is complete, additional issues that must be considered include:

1. Is there an election deadline? Is it feasible? What are the costs and benefits of possible timelines?

2. Have combatants demobilized and disarmed? Is security sufficient? How will it be addressed?

3. Is it likely that contenders will participate?

4. Is a constitution validated?

5. Is there reliable census data for establishing electoral districts?

6. Is there agreement on the legal framework?

7. Is there election administration mechanism that is independent and neutral?

8. Are all areas of the country accessible?

9. Does an environment exist to enable competition (e.g. media freedom)?

10. Are out-of-country or refugee and displaced-person voting an issue?

11. What is the budget and what financial resources are available?

12. Can international advisors and observers advise and observe?

(c) The questions in this chapter illustrate what should be asked about country context. Additionally, Civilian and military planners and policymakers should assess the political, legal, and funding context. Most importantly, the assessment should serve as a basis for USG interagency (and sometimes international) consensus on goals and set the framework for working with HN authorities during this very delicate period.

(2) **Step 2: Define the USG interagency goal in supporting an election**. Without USG consensus on a policy goal, unity of effort among all participants cannot be achieved.

For transitional elections, the likely strategic objective will be for elections to mitigate conflicts. Important factors in assessing mitigation of conflict are whether the elections include people formerly excluded because of the dynamics of the conflict, whether the spoilers are neutralized, and whether popular will is expressed. The goal should not focus on a specific election outcome, thereby providing a context for losers to boycott or resort to arms. Nor should the strategy fixate on a particular schedule, but rather, on the process of bringing people formerly engaged in violent conflict into a peaceful competition and an acceptance of the results.

(3) **Step 3: Plan for a combination of activities connected to the common USG objectives**. A strategic approach to election and political processes incorporates the full range of USG assets – whether diplomatic, assistance, economic, information, or military – toward achievement of operational objectives, which may vary from between operations. In synchronizing the various tools available to the USG, diplomacy is particularly critical to help adversaries agree on the rules of competition, deter boycotts, advocate for a peaceful pre-election environment, encourage the acceptance of results, and perhaps most importantly, ensure international community consensus on an integrated approach to support the process. Assistance should both inform and buttress USG policy by supporting the election process, political parties, and the participation of voters, and provide incentives for spoilers to join the competition and deterrents to those intent on derailing it. USG or coalition military forces may be critical to improving security, as well as providing training to HN police or auxiliary police.

(4) **Step 4: Identify a budget and how it will be resourced.** The budget should be based on the activities identified in the preceding steps. While there is no set formula for estimating an election budget, past elections in peacekeeping environments tended to cost $10-30 per registered voter. During larger, more complex operations, as in Cambodia, Mozambique, Afghanistan, and Iraq; the overall budget ran into the hundreds of millions of dollars. Smaller countries with better communications and administrative infrastructure (Central America and the Balkans) had budgets in the tens of millions of dollars. In peacekeeping environments, the cost of promoting the integrity of the electoral process (e.g., domestic monitoring, international observation, political party pollwatching, etc.) accounted for roughly half of the budget. Equally critical is to identify how the budget will be resourced and, if it requires multi-donor contributions, how those contributions can be synchronized. See http://www.aceproject.org/main/english/po/po45.htm for a sample costing worksheet prepared by the ACE Election Knowledge Network.

(5) **Step 5: Take account of interconnections between elections, political parties, and other post-conflict activities**. Peacekeeping operations are complex, with inter-related activities designed to be mutually supporting. The interconnections will vary in the different operations and from country to country. However, several types of connections are common across post-conflict activities:

(a) **Disarmament, Demobilization, and Reintegration (DDR):** In many peacekeeping situations, DDR will be underway. DDR activities can complement political party strengthening programs. For example, the disarmament, demobilization, and reintegration of former belligerents is one of the primary steps in transforming a combative force into a political party that seeks power through the ballot box instead of through force. Existing parties may also be armed, and a DDR program can help ensure their disarmament. The pace of DDR is also likely to influence the feasibility of an election date. In Angola and Cambodia, for example, holding elections without having completed DDR is often cited as a critical flaw. If delaying the election will result in a better security environment and not derail the entire peace process or invite constitutional debate, then delay may be prudent. If former belligerents are still largely armed and ready to mobilize, if there is not an effective ceasefire, if access throughout the territory is inhibited, or if relevant political forces will not participate, then elections are likely premature. In this period, efforts to create incentives for peaceful participation should be redoubled.

(b) **Political and Civil Affairs (CA):** In most stability or peacekeeping operations, there is a vital interaction with the political and civil society structures. CA units will commonly work with civil society and local governments, and they are uniquely qualified to support civil society efforts to promote democracy, monitor media coverage, and support voter information and participation programs. Including these offices and leveraging their strengths and outreach should be a part of all elections planning and strategies. Where possible, CA officers should coordinate closely with their civilian counterparts in the AMEMB, IGOs and other international organizations, and NGOs who may have the lead for engagement with the political and civil society structures.

(c) **Transitional Justice:** Truth and justice commissions are sometimes created in countries coming out of civil war, such as Sierra Leone. In other countries, such as Bosnia, war-crime tribunals may be established. The timing and mandate of these types of proceedings are usually determined in the peace agreement, but they need to be carefully considered in relation to the electoral timetable. Although a means toward reconciliation, transitional justice efforts can be divisive and adversely influence the electoral process by producing new information, resurfacing memories, or publicly placing blame and holding individuals accountable. For election purposes, it is optimal to subject potential candidates to a judicial process prior to the election. Otherwise, it falls to election bodies to determine whether individuals or groups should be allowed to compete – decisions that are better handled by justice authorities. At a minimum, timing should be coordinated so that transitional justice activities do not disrupt the electoral process or discourage former belligerents from joining the process.

GOVERNMENTAL RESPONSIBILITY TO HOLD FREE AND FAIR ELECTIONS

Since World War II, the international community has established by treaty[119] the principle that every citizen should have the right and opportunity: 1) to take part in the conduct of public affairs, directly or through freely elected representatives; 2) to vote and to be elected at genuine periodic elections which shall be by universal and equal suffrage and shall be by secret ballot, guaranteeing the free expression of the will of the electors; and 3) to have access, on general terms of equality, to the country's public services. In furtherance of these rights, a number of international bodies have developed detailed election standards. One authoritative set of election commitments is found in the 1990 Copenhagen Document agreed by the participating states of the Organization for Security and Cooperation in Europe (OSCE), under which the 56 OSCE participating states in Europe, Central Asia, and North America are committed to:

(1) hold free elections at reasonable intervals, as established by law; permit all seats in at least one chamber of the national legislature to be freely contested in a popular vote;

(2) guarantee universal and equal suffrage to adult citizens;

(3) ensure that votes are cast by secret ballot or by equivalent free voting procedure, and that they are counted and reported honestly with the official results made public;

(4) respect the right of citizens to seek political or public office, individually or as representatives of political parties or organizations, without discrimination;

(5) respect the right of individuals and groups to establish, in full freedom, their own political parties or other political organizations and provide such political parties and organizations with the necessary legal guarantees to enable them to compete with each other on a basis of equal treatment before the law and by the authorities;

(6) ensure that law and public policy work to permit political campaigning to be conducted in a fair and free atmosphere in which neither administrative action, violence nor intimidation bars the parties and the candidates from freely presenting their views and qualifications, or prevents the voters from learning and discussing them or from casting their vote free of fear of retribution;

(7) provide that no legal or administrative obstacle stands in the way of unimpeded access to the media on a nondiscriminatory basis for all political groupings and individuals wishing to participate in the electoral process; and

(8) ensure that candidates who obtain the necessary number of votes required by law are duly installed in office and are permitted to remain in office until their term expires or is otherwise brought to an end in a manner that is regulated by law in conformity with democratic parliamentary and constitutional procedures.

3. Operational Planning for Elections

a. Part 1: The Election Cycle

(1) Following conclusion of a conflict, local and international authorities are often pressured to organize elections to legitimate governing structures and to demonstrate democratic progress. As mentioned previously, while there is serious debate on the wisdom of early elections, the potential benefit of elections as the way to contain formerly violent disputes also entices citizens wearied by conflict as well as the international community. However, there are important potential downsides to organizing elections after a conflict. Transitional elections carry a high risk of institutionalizing winner-take-all arrangements, encouraging zero-sum thinking, igniting violence, and reinforcing destabilizing social divisions, particularly if the proper groundwork for elections has not been established systematically.

(2) Systematic election planning can help reduce risks associated with transitional elections. In this context, it is critical to successful election operations for military planners to understand the stages in an election cycle and the basic role that military may take at each stage. The seven stages to an election listed below have been adopted from a similar list proposed by Major Timothy Barrick[120], USMC, as an operational framework for military support to elections, based on analysis of the role of the US military in support of the 2004 presidential elections in Afghanistan. Direct support to elections will vary depending on the stage of the election being supported. As correctly noted by Major Barrick, while the military should not be directly involved in the actual mechanics of each of these stages, it is critical that the military be aware of the ongoing process so that operations can be synchronized with election activities and directly contribute to their success. It is also important that the military be aware of the potential for fraud and corruption of the electoral process in each of the stages. The military should be prepared to support the HN and IGO and other international organizations in their efforts to mitigate fraud and to assure the conduct of a secure, transparent and verifiable election.

(a) **Stage 1: Establishment of the Legal Framework**. In a constitutional democracy, the structure of the government, the rules for the formation of political parties and eligibility for public office, and the procedures for the conduct of an election are established in laws and regulations that define the legal framework for the election. The two key elements in this framework are the constitution and the election law. When this framework is deficient, the national legislature or parliament must adopt laws to fill the gaps, often drawing on the advice of expert advisors supplied by the international community.

(b) **Stage 2: Voter Registration**. One of the first requirements in any election process is the registration of the voting population. This serves many purposes but is particularly critical for determining the logistical requirements of the election: the locations of polling centers, the quantities of election materials, and the number of election workers required. Compiling this database (and producing voter IDs) is one of the most arduous and expensive tasks of the election process and in a post-conflict environment is frequently complicated by the destruction of records in the course of the conflict.

(c) **Stage 3: Electoral System and Political Party Preparations**. This stage of the election process is primarily aimed at establishing the political and institutional framework for the election. This involves the creation of an election management commission, the raising of funds from donor countries, the recruitment and training of election workers, the determination of voting districts, the locations of polling centers, the formation of political parties, the conduct of civic education efforts, the determination of political candidates, and the conduct of election campaigning by candidates and parties. Due to its highly political nature, the military has almost no direct involvement in this stage outside that of shaping the overall security environment in the country. However, it is critical for the military to establish coordination mechanisms with key electoral officials as election planning is ongoing throughout this process. While candidate security is a prime concern during the election campaigning period, US forces will generally leave this task to indigenous security forces in all but extreme circumstances, since having foreign forces visibly protecting candidates can send negative messages to the populace regarding the viability of HN security forces and the influence of foreign powers in the election.

(d) **Stage 4: Distribution of Election Materials and Information**. The distribution of election materials to polling stations and information to the public marks a significant shift into high gear for election operations. It begins the final countdown to election day and is an intense logistics effort that will frequently require assistance from military forces. The distribution of voting materials involves two categories : sensitive (ballot papers, forms for reporting voting station results, and inkbottles) and non-sensitive (empty ballot boxes, polling screens, and furniture). Publicizing voting details (process, eligibility, locations, etc.,) is also a key to good voter turnout and a successful election.

(e) **Stage 5: Conducting the Vote**. The actual Election Day is the seminal event of the election process. Due to the voting population's vulnerability to attack, it is also the most critical stage, when election and security operations must be closely synchronized. Depending on the security situation, Election Day and the days that immediately precede and follow it, may be a time for the considered use of surge operations to establish presence and area security dominance in key population centers.

(f) **Stage 6: Collection and Counting of Ballots**. Once voting is completed, a second major logistical effort is initiated to move ballots from polling stations to either counting centers or district election commission headquarters. In most cases, the election commission at the polling center will count the ballots, then send a summary of the results and the used ballots under seal to the district election commission, which the results are tabulated with those coming in from other polling stations. In some cases, such as Afghanistan in 2004, conditions may require that ballots be transported to a counting center at the district or provincial level. In either case, ballots and other sensitive election materials must be secured by election workers and police. During this stage military forces may need to focus on route security and monitoring the security of the polling stations or counting centers while ballots are tabulated.

(g) **Stage 7: Announcement of Election Results and Installment of Winners into Office**. The final step in the election process is the announcement of election results and the entry of newly elected officials into office. This stage is critical in that the election results must be viewed by the populace as legitimate. There is also a danger that election losers may resort to violence. Military planners must, therefore, develop contingency plans for dealing with widespread violence by election losers.

WHO ARE THE MAIN PARTICIPANTS IN AN ELECTION?

In addition to political parties/candidates and voters themselves, it is essential for there to be an **election authority** to organize the election; this authority may be either indigenous or composed of representatives of intergovernmental and other international organizations, or some combination. Election authorities are generally organized into multiple levels with some form of a **central election commission** at the national level, district election commissions that tabulate election results at the sub-national or district level, and **precinct election commissions** that administer polling stations and count ballots that have been cast. Others key participants in the election process include:

Groups that monitor the election process. As a general rule, these groups should be encouraged to become active as early in the process as possible. Some may require international support for their activities. They include:

(1) **Domestic election monitoring organizations** may exist or may emerge from other types of organizations to monitor voter, party and candidate registration, to track media access and political party conduct, to conduct parallel vote tabulations or quick counts, and to monitor voting, counting. Domestic political party observers may also be present during the election process to look out for their party's concerns.

(2) **International observers** are usually helpful in drawing the widest attention to the electoral process, preventing intimidation in susceptible areas, and lending credibility where domestic capacity is limited or biased. International observers may be sent by the United Nations or by regional bodies, such as the African Union, the British Commonwealth, the European Union, the Organization for Security and Cooperation in Europe (OSCE), or the Organization of American States (OAU). **Electoral grievance bodies** play a critical role in adjudicating election disputes.

(3) **The media**, which can report on the election process and highlight progress or abuses.

Groups to encourage participation and educate voters, including civic education organizations to educate voters and conduct get-out-the-vote campaigns, journalists to provide information to citizens about the election as well as candidates and parties, and social networks, such as parent teacher associations and women's groups, that have an interest in their members participating in the election. Some groups will also require outside support to conduct their activities.

Groups that oppose elections and who could resist or try to spoil the election must be identified, understood, and their potential actions addressed in the overall election strategy. These can include armed combatants, militia tied to a political party or faction, organized crime groups, incumbent political leaders and political or economic elites who stand to lose power elections, host-nation émigrés, and neighboring countries or populations in neighboring countries that benefited from the conflict.

b. **Part 2: Establishing a Security Concept of Operations**

(1) The second step in operational planning for an election is to establish a security concept of operations. Such a concept of operations should reflect the status of any security sector reform efforts that are underway in the HN. Pre-existing security forces – whether from military, police, or nonstate sources – are often agents of one faction or another and in some cases are sources of extrajudicial human rights violations. As part of election security preparations, international peacekeepers, local security forces, and other security providers should be properly coordinated and each must be capable of performing their assigned role during the election process. Since newly established security forces will lack experience and may not be reliable when confronted with a politically charged election atmosphere, the credibility of the nascent or reforming security force as well as of the election itself can be at risk. A range of technical measures focused on election security can lower the pressure on new security institutions, including the use of joint operation centers, dedicated training on security, weapon exclusion zones, campaign cooling-off periods, and codes of conflict (see http://aceproject.org/ace-en/focus/elections-and-security).

(2) The security concept of operations is also important because the electoral process can provide tempting, soft targets for spoilers. Electoral administrators, political parties, and the electorate can be targeted for violence or intimidation. Electoral sites and warehouses can be attacked, while access to polling stations or campaign sites can be disrupted by violence. The election process can be sabotaged from within as well as from without. There is usually a tendency for such attacks to escalate as an election approaches. A comprehensive electoral security strategy should be thought through well in advance and adapted as circumstances evolve. In situations where there are joint forces or international peacekeepers, local forces should provide the inner perimeter of security, supported and coordinated by joint forces or by international security forces, such as the UN civilian police or troops. Local and international security forces should receive training on their appropriate conduct and responses during the process and on the presence and roles of the press, observers, and monitors at electoral sites and polls.

(3) **In formulating the security concept of operations, it is extremely important to take into account the special political and cultural environment in which joint forces will be operating.** While the presence of uniformed personnel can assert an aura of authority that is useful in preventing or quelling civil violence, the projection of the same aura in locations associated with elections can be perceived as an effort to intimidate voters and interfere in the election process. Accordingly, an operational security plan must clearly define limits on the extent to which uniformed military personnel can be seen in polling stations or have physical contact with ballots and other sensitive election materials.

4. Military Tasks in Post-Conflict Elections

a. The basic military competencies required to support post-conflict elections are planning; providing security, logistics, and transportation; gathering and analyzing intelligence and information; conducting PA and populace outreach; and supporting law development. JTF planners should anticipate that some military tasks will need to be executed continuously through the entire election process while others will only be required during one or more of the seven election stages discussed above. To simplify the presentation of this section, tasks are organized by election phase, beginning with tasks that must be carried out across all phases of an election, then presenting specific tasks that need to be executed in the pre-election, election campaign and voting, and post-election phases of the election process. While it should be anticipated that joint forces will be mainly concerned with security and logistics tasks, in some cases they may be needed to perform tasks that support HN, USG, and other international civilian agencies election efforts if and when a hostile or uncertain environment precludes these bodies from operating.

(1) **Tasks in All Phases of the Election Process**

(a) **Security**

$\underline{1}$. Deter and defeat threats to the election process that may occur before, during, and after the election.

$\underline{2}$. Support the rebuilding, reform, and expansion of indigenous security forces.

$\underline{3}$. Coordinate and integrate security operations and planning with those of HN security forces and election officials.

$\underline{4}$. Secure key election facilities where ballots and other sensitive election materials are produced and stored, teaming with HN security forces, if capable and available.

(b) **Logistics**. Provide logistics support for key election events.

(c) **Public Communication**

$\underline{1}$. Provide public information and civic education in coordination with the AMEMB and the HN election authority.

$\underline{2}$. Support and monitor media coverage of the election. Correct any misinformation or disinformation related to the election being disseminated to the public.

(d) **Intelligence and Information Gathering**. Provide J2 intelligence on threats to elections to HN and other relevant participants.

(e) **Stakeholder Coordination**. Participate in principals, donors, implementing agencies coordination fora.

(2) **Tasks in the Pre-Election Phase**

(a) **Security**

1. Establish a working relationship with the HN security sector (police as well as military); the US embassy should be able to provide advice and help establish contacts with HN authorities.

2. Conduct a pre-election security assessment, preferably in cooperation with HN authorities.

3. Coordinate election security planning and operations with HN authorities and participate in (and, if necessary, help to establish) election security planning groups at the national, subnational/provincial, and local/municipal levels.

4. Establish and staff a joint election security operations group.

5. Establish or ensure lines of communication are at all levels, from the operations center down to individual polling places.

6. Preparing daily election threat analyses.

7. Identifying election security "hot spots" or "watch areas."

8. Establishing a plan for protection of election workers, election materials, registration, observers, and voting/ballot counting sites.

9. Organizing training and rehearsals for security operations.

10. Ensuring safe movement of media personnel during the election season.

11. Ensuring the security for ballots and voting materials during printing and pre-election storage.

12. Conducting security briefings for international observers.

13. Developing emergency and evacuation procedures for observers and identify "no go" areas.

14. Planning for crowd control and potential disturbances at polls.

15. Establishing a plan for securely storing ballots/ballot boxes following the vote count and while the overall results are being tabulated, validated, and certified.

16. Protect mobile voter education and outreach workers.

(b) **Establishing a Legal and Institutional Framework for Elections**

1. Analyze the peace agreement ending the conflict and any relevant UN resolutions for guidance and requirements that would affect the conduct of transitional elections.

2. Assess the need for changing the laws and regulations governing the conduct of elections and, if necessary, provide expert advisors to the legislative committee(s) drafting or revising the election law.

3. Protect government officials and facilities involved in the development of a new legal framework for elections.

4. Provide election experts, generally military and civilian counsel and CA, to election legal working groups, if needed.

5. Support the establishment of commissions to adjudicate election complaints.

(c) Voter Registration and Credentialing (e.g., ID cards)

1. Develop a concept of operations for supporting voter registration and synchronize security operations with registration efforts.

2. Support public information campaigns to inform citizens about registering and encourage their participation in the electoral process.

3. Provide logistical and security support to possibly thousands of voter registration sites and to mobile registration teams.

4. Assist registration teams in gaining access to remote or high-threat areas.

5. Monitor voter registration mobile teams and registration of nomad, armed forces, internally displaced persons (IDPs), and refugees.

(d) Electoral System and Political Party Preparations

1. Support establishment of election facilities (offices and polling centers) at the local, regional, and national levels.

2. Train recruited electoral workers.

3. Establish liaison with key election security and logistics planning nodes at the national and sub-national levels.

4. Monitor candidate security, noting any private security arrangements.

5. Link election field offices to forward operating bases, provincial reconstruction teams, or comparable US military structures that be deployed in the election area.

6. Support and secure the distribution of sensitive election materials (ballot papers, official voter registration lists, and protocol forms for reporting election results) by authorized election workers.

7. Support distribution of non-sensitive election materials, if needed.

(e) **Operational Election Planning**

1. Provide planners to assist the election authority.

2. Develop a military election support plan that includes security, PA, civic outreach, logistics, communications, and civilian coordination sub-plans.

3. Establish military liaisons to AMEMB and UN election teams as well as to relevant HN working groups (security, PA, outreach, logistics).

4. Coordinate with election authority in security plan development.

5. Establish joint planning groups that include all relevant ministries.

6. Plan for election operations center (joint elections security center may be co-located).

7. Plan use of, and work with, private security contractors — operations/logistics/security/medical support.

8. Prepare budget and funding requests.

9. Assess threats and anticipate actions to disrupt elections, including plans to mitigate election fraud.

10. Publicize the vote to gain legitimacy.

(f) **HN Security Force Training and Mentoring**

1. Develop a plan for building the capacity of security forces (police and military).

2. Provide election-specific training for security forces, including principles or best practices in maintaining public order, PA, and conduct at polling stations, counting centers, and other election sites.

3. Assist security forces (police and military) with establishing transparent and accountable rules for procurement of commodities.

4. Conduct rapid action training.

<u>5</u>. Train police for crowd control.

<u>6</u>. Prepare security forces to assist in logistics planning and movement of materials.

<u>7</u>. Plan for post-election evaluation of security forces.

(g) **Civic Outreach and Public Information**

<u>1</u>. Citizens and candidates are informed about election deadlines, regulations, and requirements and encouraged to participate.

<u>2</u>. Rebuild critical media infrastructure for election communication.

<u>3</u>. Identify, establish, and protect (as needed) outlets for news media.

<u>4</u>. Participate in and cross-functional or cross-agency public communication coordination group to improve public messaging and leverage communication assets.

<u>5</u>. Issue press releases supporting election authority's daily talking points.

<u>6</u>. Provide public outreach messaging, in support of election authority's public information effort.

<u>7</u>. Develop provincial/regional public messaging with HN.

<u>8</u>. Coordinate with election authority and donors to establish election media center.

<u>9</u>. Provide training/mentoring to journalists and media professionals as needed.

<u>10</u>. Control for misinformation and disinformation.

<u>11</u>. Monitor public opinion.

<u>12</u>. Support development of HN security forces' public communication capabilities.

<u>13</u>. Support civic education campaigns concerning the elections, including election deadlines, regulations, and requirements, and encourage citizens to participate.

<u>14</u>. Develop election education outreach for both HN security forces and civilian audiences.

<u>15</u>. Provide logistic support to civic outreach and public information efforts.

<u>16</u>. Provide posters, radios, radio stations, and other military communication assets for election authority use, if needed.

<u>17</u>. Assist in distribution of voter education materials, if needed.

(3) **Tasks during Voting**

(a) **Distribution and Protection of Election Materials**

<u>1</u>. Support election day logistics efforts, if needed.

<u>2</u>. In the hours following the completion of voting, support HN security forces in protecting polling stations and other locations where votes are being counted and election results are being tabulated.

<u>3</u>. Support authorized election officials in securing and transporting sensitive election materials (ballots, voter registration lists, and completed protocols transmitting the vote count results to higher-level election bodies) following voting.

<u>4</u>. Escort authorized election officials who are transporting ballots and boxes, preferably in the presence of observers, to district election commission headquarters.

(b) **Election Day Security**

<u>1</u>. Conduct area security in key population centers and along lines of communication.

<u>2</u>. Stand up quick reaction forces with coverage of key population centers.

<u>3</u>. Monitor progress of elections and reports of violence, interference with voters, or disruption of established voting and counting procedures at polling stations, counting centers, or at district or national election commission headquarters.

(c) **Election Observation, Monitoring, and Supervision**

<u>1</u>. Provide assistance in the development of security plans to IGO or other international organizations that are sending observers to the election and develop plans to cooperate with HN security forces and private security companies that are providing for the safe movement of observers.

<u>2</u>. Develop emergency evacuation procedures for potentially hundreds of international election observers and identify "no go" areas.

<u>3</u>. Meet and brief representatives of stakeholder and donor organizations regarding election security preparations and potential risks to international observers and other foreign civilians that are in the HN to support the elections.

(4) **Tasks Following Elections**

(a) **Collection and Storage of Ballots and Election Materials**

<u>1</u>. Secure subnational/district and national election commission headquarters where vote counts are being tabulated and election results validated.

<u>2</u>. Provide security and storage/archiving for voted ballots and other election materials.

<u>3</u>. Secure the facilities where ballots are stored while election results are being validated.

(b) **Announcement of Election Results**. Respond to violent reactions by election losers, if needed.

(c) **Inauguration**. Support HN security forces protecting inauguration events, if needed.

(d) **Evaluation and After-Action Reviews**. Organize security forces after-election reviews and evaluation.

5. Planning Considerations

a. **Considerations in all Phases of the Election Process**

(1) **Planners should take the cultural context of the election into account**. For example, elections should be conducted in a way that maximizes the participation of women and other traditionally marginalized groups. In some countries, arrangements to separate men and women may be necessary (e.g. voter registration and polling sites).

(2) **Plan for an integrated process, but also for the different phases of the electoral cycle, including the pre-election, election-day, and the post-election periods**. To the extent possible, assistance programs should have a long-term sustainability focus so that the institutions and capacity built last through subsequent elections. Minimize dependence on external advisors and avoid the introduction of expensive equipment and technology so that appropriate, cost-effective, and sustainable long-term systems are developed.

(3) **Plan for unexpected events that require surge capacity, whether financial ors human**. The election process is rarely smooth, and unanticipated delays and changes are common. To reduce the risks associated with unanticipated developments, a contingency response fund should be set up. Among the contingencies this could help

support are unanticipated run-off elections or referendums. Delays in electoral calendars almost always result in increased costs for election administration and associated processes.

(4) Threat information is critically important to all donors, IGOs or other international organizations, and NGOs supporting the elections. It also is a positive way to establish good civilian-military relations.

b. **Pre-Election Phase**

(1) **Establishment of an election complaints and appeals unit is critical.** It links citizens to the election process; provides legal recourse for complaints, reduces the possibility of violent conflict, and increases the legitimacy of the electoral process. However, the legal framework is usually new and will be severely tested in the complaints process. It is imperative to have attorneys from a variety of traditions work together in establishing process, regulations and decisions. For a credible complaints and appeals process, it is vital to recruit and train investigators.

(2) **An interagency, multilateral cooperation plan is important to coordinate donor activities.** A plan is needed to establish a clear structure, division of labor, and common agenda among donors and technical experts, thereby ensuring that programs and advisors are not working at cross-purposes and that certain activities or civil society organizations are not overwhelmed by international assistance. In many cases local groups will be financially and technically dependent on international support and unable to steel themselves against competing donor agendas. Technical assistance should be provided where possible on the counterpart system to build the capacity of the local election administrators and their staff and to ensure local ownership of the process.

(3) **Liaison requirements may be extensive.** There are typically multiple strategic, operational and tactical election working groups. These may include the HN election commission and ministries of defense and interior, the AMEMB, the UN, and other military forces. In addition to organizational liaisons, there will also be functional working groups (security, PA, outreach, and donor coordination) to which military liaisons should be appointed.

(4) **Coordinate activities and budgets with on members of the international community.** The international community is most effective when it works together and when the actions are complementary. In some elections, support to the elections and political parties will be channeled through one mechanism, such as a UN Trust Fund. This can provide for an integrated effort and avoid duplication. In other cases, donor funding is provided bilaterally to joint or separate projects. These programs should be coordinated through donor meetings, usually chaired by the UN. If funding is provided through a multilateral mechanism, it is essential to have a clear understanding of how this funding is controlled and allocated. In many cases, the USG will contribute both bilaterally and multilaterally, as many multilateral trust funds do not allow for a donor to allocate funds to a particular activity.

(5) Approaching elections will usually require additional military forces; planning for rotations during this period should include time for new arrivals to receive adequate orientation on election tasks.

(6) Election planning should take account of special needs and external voters, for example, members of the HN's military, IDPs, nomads, and citizens returning for the election from outside the country.

(7) Private contractors are increasingly being used during post-conflict elections to provide security for facilities and candidates, and more importantly to provide field operational linkages between election authorities and multinational forces.

(8) Consider geographic phasing of voter registration so that security resources can be concentrated if HN security forces are not to full capacity – "rolling elections."

(9) It is critical that ballots are secured before and after the voting; otherwise allegations of ballot duplication and fraud can undermine the election's legitimacy and credibility.

(10) In many post-conflict elections, voter registration cards are issued and become a powerful symbol of a country's new beginning. However, the drive for a symbolic "new beginning" should not so rigorously pursued so as to make it difficult to vote for rural voters or voters in isolated regions who have alternative but to use older forms of identification.

(11) Voter registration can serve as a temporary substitute for a census. Conducting a new census is always controversial in a conflict zone because of implications about ethnic/religious status and rights of citizenship.

(12) Duplicating and selling voter cards becomes a primary concern during elections. Technological advances will eventually limit voter card fraud by embedding non-transferrable, non-duplicating information.

(13) Security force development for elections should be incorporated as part of a broader plan for governance-strengthening and HN institutional development, at both the national (interior and defense ministries) and local levels.

(14) In a first post-conflict election, US military forces often have to provide security and communications equipment, vehicles, and other commodities for the conduct a safe election. Plan on deficiencies and be prepared to provide equipment as necessary.

(15) **Assistance to HN entities should avoid large capital purchases and focus on appropriate technology.** Keep technology acquisitions transparent and locally-appropriate. Large procurements are also opportunities for patronage and graft, and some systems and equipment purchased can be inappropriate for local conditions or are unsustainable for local election management bodies.

(16) During the election campaign, the US Embassy (political officers, USAID DG officers, etc.) will be monitoring and reporting on the views of candidates and political party platforms. Information developed through military channels will be of interest to the Embassy. However, care should be exercised in contact with candidates and political parties so as to avoid creating the impression of US interference in the electoral process.

c. **Election Phase**

(1) Large money contracts for activities such as printing ballots and transportation are ripe for fraud, graft and corruption. Developing anti-corruption measures is necessary.

(2) Ballots must be secured before and after voting by duly authorized election officials in a manner that prevents tampering, since ballot duplication and fraud can undermine an election's legitimacy and credibility.

(3) If joint forces assist in the transportation of ballots, it is crucial that authorized civilian election officials and, if possible, independent observers accompany the ballots to guard against accusations of ballot tampering.

(4) In a high profile election, hundreds or thousands of international election observers may arrive days before the voting. At a minimum, the organizations supplying observers will request meetings with US embassy and joint force representatives, desire security briefings, and may erroneously believe that multinational forces will provide personal security for their delegations. Observer groups often represent a country or IGO and will expect their troops to assist.

d. **Post-Election Phase**

(1) Election security needs do not end on voting day. Post-election presents several security challenges. Counting, the announcement of winners and losers, and the inauguration of new political leaders are prime disruption opportunities.

(2) Too often after an election, international staff may quickly depart the country and attention turns away from the elections. There is a limited opportunity to facilitate the gathering of election staff to conduct after action evaluations and collect lessons learned and best practices.

6. **Key Agencies and Implementing Partners**

a. **US Government Stakeholders**

(1) If functioning, the **AMEMB** in the HN is generally the best source of up-to-date information on HN conditions and can be instrumental in helping JFCs establish contact with HN authorities for purposes of election planning. In developing countries, the interagency "country team" at the embassy typically includes at least one political officer who can advise on the political and cultural context of elections, a press and culture section that can provide information on the condition of the media and journalism

in the country, as well as a USAID mission. These offices will also have information on US election assistance programs underway in the HN and are the best point at which to begin gathering information on the status of any election-related programs that are being conducted in the country by other foreign government donors, intergovernmental organization, or nongovernmental organizations. In addition, the economic and commercial sections of an embassy (which may be combined at smaller posts) can advise on the economic dimensions of the election. Members of the country team maintain regular contact with HN government officials dealing with their respective areas. A listing of key officers at AMEMBs worldwide can be found on the State Department's web site, http://www.state.gov.

(2) **USAID** implements election and other assistance programs through "implementing partners," which may be HN organizations, other USG departments or agencies, IGOs, NGOs, or contractors. A number of offices within USAID headquarters in Washington, DC are closely involved with support to elections. (http://www.usaid.gov)

(a) The **Democracy and Governance Office** (DCHA/DG) provides technical, programmatic, financial, strategic and TDY personnel in support of free elections.

(b) The **Office of Transition Initiatives** (DCHA/OTI) assists with election information dissemination and election commission support.

(c) The **Office of Conflict Management and Mitigation** (DCHA/CMM) works with adapting elections and governance program to conflict environments.

(3) Many bureaus and offices within the **Department of State** (DOS) are also involved directly or indirectly in supporting democratic elections. Those with a most direct role include:

(a) The **Bureau of Democracy, Human Rights and Labor** (DRL), which can support democratic elections by funding technical assistance and training.

(b) The **Office of the Coordinator for Reconstruction and Stabilization** (S/CRS), which is responsible for interagency coordination and development of strategic plans. Elections are a component of post-conflict reconstruction and stabilization activities.

(c) The **Bureau of International Narcotics and Law Enforcement** (INL) has a connection to election security through its assistance and training programs for the police and security sector development.

(d) **Regional bureaus** provide policy guidance and backup to embassies.

b. **Intergovernmental Organizations**

(1) The **United Nations**, through several of its departments and specialized agencies, usually plays an important role in elections. Specific UN organizations involved in elections include:

(a) The **UN Electoral Assistance Division** (UNEAD) assists with voter education and participation and conducts needs assessments, election administration, technical assistance, monitoring and observation, and verification and supervision. It may work directly or through UNDP or peacekeeping operations. UNEAD falls under the authority of the UN Department of Political Affairs. (www.un.org/depts/dpa/ead)

(b) The **UN Development Program** (UNDP) supports the conduct of democratic elections, works with political parties and provides voter education. It assists with technical, programmatic, financial, commodities, and donor coordination. (www.undp.org)

(c) The **UN Department of Economic and Social Affairs** (UN DESA) works closely with UNDP, providing technical backup at the UN. (www.unpan.org/dpepa.asp)

(d) The **UN Department of Peacekeeping Operations** (UN DPKO) handles electoral and political components of peacekeeping operations. Its specific role will depend on its mandate and may be comprehensive. (www.un.org)

(e) The **UN Office for Project Services** (UNOPS) offers election assistance and can support the conduct of a census. It may support technical election operations, planning, procurement, commodities and logistics. (www.unops.org)

(2) The **European Union** (EU) supports democratic elections, political parties, and voter education/participation through the provision of technical, commodity and financial assistance as well as election observers. Funding decisions may take a long time. (www.europa.eu.int/comm)

(3) The **European Commission for Democracy through Law** (Venice Commission) can offer legal drafting and opinions, training, and technical assistance to election management bodies and courts. (www.venice.coe.int)

(4) **International IDEA** can provide assessments, studies and manuals for democratic election, political parties and voter education/participation. (www.idea.int)

(5) The **Organization for Security and Cooperation in Europe** (OSCE), through its **Office of Democratic Institutions and Human Rights** (ODIHR), offers support for democratic elections to its 56 participating states. ODHIR deploys election observation missions to assess the implementation of OSCE election commitments in participating states, but has on invitation participated in election missions outside the OSCE region, for example, sending a team to the August 2009 Afghan parliamentary elections. ODHIR also conducts technical assistance projects and legislative reviews. (www.osce.org/odihr)

(6) The **Organization of American States** (OAS) offers technical, financial, commodity assistance to elections, political parties and voter education/participation through a special unit for the promotion of democracy. It can also provide election observers and monitors. (www.oas.org)

c. **Other National Development Agencies**

(1) There are several other nations that may have programs to assist elections in post-conflict situations. These include the UK's Department for International Development (DFID) and the Canadian International Development Agency (CIDA). Most foreign ministries and aid organizations, however, conduct their election support activities through HN organizations, IGOs, NGOs, or contractors. Contact information for the major national development agencies can be found in Appendix D, "References and Web Sites For Key Stakeholders, Donors, and Implementing Partners."

(2) The **Australian Election Commission** can assist with election administration, information technology, training and other technical assistance. Usually funded by AusAid, the Commission has developed a training program (BRIDGE) in cooperation with the UN and IFES. (www.aec.gov.au)

(3) **Elections Canada** provides technical expertise, usually through the Canadian International Development Agency (CIDA), for democratic elections, and voter education/participation. It has a large pool of electoral experts available for contracting. (www.elections.ca)

(4) The **Federal Electoral Institute** (Mexico) an offer short-term, small scale technical expertise for democratic elections. (www.ife.org.mx)

d. **Nongovernmental Organizations and Implementing Partners**

(1) The **International Foundation for Electoral Systems** (IFES) offers technical and procurement assistance as well as support for civil societies. (www.ifes.org)

(2) The **National Democratic Institute for International Affairs** (NDI) offers international election observation and supports the electoral integrity efforts of political parties and domestic nonpartisan election monitoring organizations. NDI also supports constitutional and law reform efforts to enhance the basis for genuine, democratic elections. (http://www.ndi.org)

(3) The **International Republican Institute** (IRI) provides practical assistance to civic and political leaders worldwide to advance democratic values practices, including democratic elections. IRI has an active program of election monitoring. (http://www.iri.org)

(4) The **Carter Center** supports democratic elections worldwide by providing observers as well as electoral mediation. (www.cartercenter.org)

(5) The **Westminster Foundation for Democracy** (WFD) is sponsored by the United Kingdom's Foreign and Commonwealth Office and provides political party election support as well as programs to educate citizens about voting and electoral systems. (www.wfd.org)

(6) **America's Development Foundation** (ADF) encourages increased citizen participation in electoral processes through support for local NGO voter education and

get-out-the-vote programs. ADF also assists local NGOs gain experience as nonpartisan election observers and poll-watchers. (http://www.adfusa.org)

(7) **Search for Common Ground** assists in developing radio and television studios that produce news, features, drama, and music, all of which are sometimes used to support the conduct of democratic elections. (http://www.sfcg.org)

(8) The **Asia Foundation** (TAF) provides technical assistance, civil society support and monitoring/observation for democratic elections in Asia. (www.asiafoundation.org)

(9) **Democracy International** offers technical, procurement, civil society support, and monitoring for democratic elections. (www.democracyinternational.us)

CHAPTER IV
MILITARY SUPPORT TO MEDIA DEVELOPMENT AND INFORMATION DISSEMINATION

1. Overview

Information in the public domain can be a powerful tool for the manipulation of perceptions, inducement of fear, increasing polarization and separation between groups, and ultimately, incitement and mobilization of populations to action and violence, which can undermine reconstruction and stabilization operations. Many of our adversaries are adept at manipulating information about US activities and spreading it via the Internet or conventional media. Just as public information can undermine reconstruction and stabilization efforts; it also can play a critical role in supporting reconstruction and stabilization activities by keeping people informed about progress and important events (elections, humanitarian relief efforts, etc.). The social, political, and economic environment of the conflict shapes the potential role of the media.

2. The Military Challenge

a. In reconstruction and stabilization operations, an effective communications strategy is a political and operational necessity. The USG response to a failed, failing or crisis state may enjoy initial worldwide support, but without an effective and consistent public information program, support can quickly turn to apathy and even opposition. An aggressive public information program plays a crucial role in explaining the presence of US personnel and the overall objectives to the local population, local and international media, the donor community, coalition or international partner states, agencies, and NGOs; keeping them abreast of progress and obstacles in the reconstruction and stabilization process and building support for the operation's activities.

b. Credible and accurate information can be rare in conflict or post-conflict environments. "The public may perceive USG official sources of information [such as the DOD-launched Iraqi Media Network] as instruments of propaganda and there may be little or no tradition of an independent, non-partisan media. Journalists may be biased in their reporting or intimidated into self-censorship, [or they may be untrained, undisciplined, and easily manipulated]. People who seek out sources of independent information may face persecution.[121] On the one hand, JFCs need to encourage independent media that offers objective information that HN populations understand and accept, media that conforms to society and local culture that is trusted. On the other hand, JFCs need to ensure that the media is not coerced or co-opted by elements opposed to the re-establishment of a legitimate and responsible government. The JFC may encounter situations where some of the media is directly or indirectly government controlled and co-exists with purely "private" media which can be newspapers or radio/TV stations established by private interests for purposes that mix both the political and informational programming.

3. Media Assessment

a. During the initial assessment for re-establishing governance, there should be a concerted effort to understand the structure and dynamics of the specific media environment as well as other sources of information available to the population. The JFC can also rely on organic public affairs (PA), information operations, and intelligence personnel to assess the information environment and media capability specific to the HN and the region. From the basis of this understanding, the JFC can then assess the potential for spoilers as well as the joint force to inform and influence information consumers or support the public information activities of the DOS, USAID, UN, or other international organizations. In addition, The JFC must also simultaneously support broader USG, UN, and coalition initiatives to support HN efforts to build media capacity through media infrastructure repair or development.

MEDIA ASSESSMENT

1.   Identify the media outlets in the country, including their audience size, circulation and sources of income, political alignment, organization, and distribution.

2.   Identify credible, effective sources of information for each audience (television, radio, print, Internet, local political/religious leaders, etc.)

3.   Identify the role that major media outlets played with respect to the conflict, the government, and post-conflict stabilization and reconstruction plans and operation.

4.   Assess the professional qualifications of journalists and identify and prioritize needs for professional development. Explore possibilities for peace journalism and building new outlets.

5.   Identify technical structure supporting media systems.

6.   Identify and prioritize emergency repairs needed for media outlets to resume operation.

7.   Identify the major Internet content providers and their audience as well as their role with respect to the conflict.

8.   Identify efforts by government or other outside interests to control or influence.

9.   Identify media regulatory environment, libel, laws and regulations that limit the freedom of the media.

10.   Identify weaknesses in the government bodies that regulate the media. Weaknesses may include corruption, political and commercial influence, and technical incompetence.

---

b. Beyond the initial assessment, there will be a requirement for on-going media-monitoring to assess the effectiveness of USG and joint force public information activities and to identify disinformation, misinformation, and propaganda and plan and execute counter activities. Continuous monitoring and assessment is also essential to support future planning.

c. Currently, there are standard assessment formats for a range of topics, such as humanitarian assessment, military tactical assessment, and legal systems assessment. Although there is no standard format available for media assessment, there are media assessment tools available (such as those used by USAID) that provide a framework for the details of a media assessment. However, in addition to the details of the media systems themselves, joint force planners need to understand link between the media and the dynamics of conflict. The following questions and background may help planners in this effort.

(1) How is the media controlled and shaped, by political and economic factors and specific factions or individuals? Who has "voice" in society, and who is silent?

Background: The American social commentator Henry Mencken said that "Freedom of the press is limited to those who own one." This acerbic, but not inaccurate, comment highlights a central issue in media assessment in post-conflict environments: How is the extant media linked to, and shaped by, larger political and economic structures? Any media system is shaped by a set of political and economic influences, and this system of influences shapes the impact of the media on the political environment.

(2) How does the population get its information? What audiences are reached?

Background: While the use of the Internet is second nature to people in developed countries and citizens in most cities and large towns in developing countries have access, it is still beyond many, if not most, rural communities in developing regions of the world. Even "Internet Cafes" when available are neither reliable nor widespread. Newspapers are found in cities and the larger towns only and, as noted earlier in this chapter, while radio stations are usually found in all countries, reception is dependent on the availability of personal radios which can be scarce. Television is another media source that is not available in many rural areas. Often tribal and communal communities rely on the chief, a leading citizen or the local religious leader for all news and opinions.

(3) To what political and operational effect?

Background: Joint force planners should assume that opposition elements will be actively disseminating their "message" to HN populations. That message will be intended to undermine and complicate the efforts of joint forces to stabilize and reconstruct society. The JFC will be challenged to distribute timely and accurate information that reaches the HN population and is considered credible in order to counter information activities of any opposition elements. As noted earlier, the challenge will be to effectively deal with opposition information activities while at the same time fostering a free and unbiased media that will not be perceived as a propaganda tool of the US forces on the ground. A balance must be found with a "local face" that the populace can identify with that can effectively counter opposition media.

d. **Media Assessment Principles**. Himelfarb offers six principles[122] that can also inform media assessment process when considered in conjunction with other material presented here and the realities on the ground:

(1) **Define the media broadly**. Adopt an expansive definition of media sector support to include information and communications technology, thereby spanning traditional media (radio, TV, print), new media (text messaging, Internet) as well as telecommunications.

(2) **Clarity of role**. Determine in advance the JFC's role in helping to provide the telecommunications infrastructure required for media development to support planning and determining requirements.

(3) **Assess infrastructure and institutions**. Telecommunications infrastructure assessments should be supplemented by assessments performed in collaboration with civilian media experts, of the media institution landscape. Such assessments are needed to inform prioritization of the expedient repairs and facilities reconstruction, as well as to provide media practitioners with essential information.

(4) **Make speed a priority**. Ensure the HN understands the USG's willingness to support the rapid development of the media sector with the funds and resources it has available. To this end, the assessment processes (infrastructure and institutions) should be pulled forward as early in the stabilization process as security allows.

(5) **Distinguish information engagement from media development**. Conflating information engagement and media development diminishes the efficacy of both. The former includes activities by the joint force and other USG agencies to disseminate timely accurate information through the most credible and effective means available to inform various audiences about reconstruction and stabilization activities; the latter about developing a media sector (e.g., radio, TV, print, Internet, telecom) that contributes to the body politic and pluralistic society.

(6) **Plan for the dual use capacity of media**. With the development of media comes the capacity to promote both peace and conflict. Mindful of this reality, infrastructure and institutional assessment supported by the joint forces in theater should incorporate credible civilian expertise on monitoring and regulation of media in support of stabilization and reconstruction.

4. Media Development

a. Redevelopment of media infrastructure and the establishment of an independent, pluralistic, and commercially sustainable media sector is critical to educating the population about reconstruction and stabilization operations. In the immediate aftermath of conflict, media outlets that remain functional may be vulnerable to pressure from individuals and groups who want to undermine reconstruction and stabilization progress, and provide those groups with a mass media platform to promote their agenda with the population. This may drive commanders to want to control media content or close the offending media outlet to ensure that the information being presented will not incite violence or undermine reconstruction and stabilization operations. This desire to censor the media must be carefully weighed against the perception of a double standard and the effect that will have on the population and their support for reconstruction and stabilization activities.

"In war-torn societies, the development of independent, pluralistic, and sustainable media is critical to fostering long-term peace and stability. Post-conflict civilian popula-tions are particularly vulnerable to manipulation by mass media as tensions run high and the possibility of violent relapse remains strong. Many civilians harbor deep skepticism and mistrust of the media, being accustomed to platforms that are controlled either by the state or by political groups looking to further their political agendas.

"An effective media strategy can mitigate postwar tensions by elevating moderate voices and dampening extremist ones. It can create peaceful channels through which differ-ences can be resolved without resort to violence. The creation of a robust media culture will also allow citizens to begin holding their government accountable for its actions and ensuring its commitment to democracy."

US Institute for Peace
Stabilization and Reconstruction Series No. 7
October 2007

b. Establishment of an independent media is not a primary responsibility of the military, but the need is very real and merits consideration by the JFC. Regardless of who has the lead for this effort, the need for military support may include personnel with a good working knowledge of the news industry as well as technical and engineering support for assisting with the rebuilding of media infrastructure. Personnel from the joint force who may be involved in rebuilding or establishing news outlets include PA, information operations (principally PSYOP) and CA.

c. Determining requirements must be based on the environment in which the reconstruction and stabilization operations are being conducted. In the spring of 2004, a CNN/USA Today/Gallup poll found that 95% of Iraqis had a working television set in their home,[123] so the potential to reach a large percentage of the people via a revitalized television network was substantial. In Afghanistan however, a 2005 survey showed that only 19% of households owned a television,[124] and so a similar effort there would have been far less effective. In regions where literacy is low, the cost benefit of establishing a substantial print media capability will be equally low.

d. Planners need to determine what can and should be done "now" and what actions need to be delayed in order to ensure success. Other considerations include:

(1) **Link any media development effort to other governance and community development efforts.**

(2) **Use community development best practices** by, with, and through, local partners.

(3) **Consider a range of options.** US media environment is <u>not</u> the model, but US media expertise can offer options. Additionally, European models of mixed state and public service broadcasters; papers aligned with political or sectarian groups; may have value.

(4) **Weigh sustainability vs. immediate need — Speed vs. quality**

(a) Desire for rapidly developing media space may be driven by information requirements.

(b) **Immediate action may undercut longer term development** if not managed in conjunction with other reconstruction and stabilization goals and objectives.

(c) **US messaging (attributed, active and passive).** Impact on media development; value and impact of US SC efforts, and impact on local media.

(d) **Development best practices balanced with principles of war.** Consider the goal of a free press and the desire to limit polarizing, destabilizing voices.

(e) **Licensing – control vs. unfettered discourse.** Consider near-term precedent for control vs. long term independence

(f) **Enforcement vs. entanglement**

<u>1</u>. Military role in media regulation and enforcement

<u>2</u>. Threshold for military involvement, mitigation

(g) **Transparency and accountability.** Dependent on local media regulatory and political environment – international and domestic accountability; accountability may be problematic in the local environment.

(h) **Promote credible voices over perceived propaganda.** US forces should enlist commercial and independent content providers to bring their own credible and diverse perspectives on HN affairs and the conflict to increasingly sophisticated and skeptical audiences. Accordingly, the JTF should consider designating funding for the development of third-party content that serves the interests of creating a public dialogue.

(i) **Recognize the value of local partners over official outlets.** The relevance of supporting the full-service studio/station model of official broadcasting may need to be reevaluated in some parts of the world. The JTF should explore developing relationships with existing media companies, channels, and brands to bring credible media to hard-to-reach audiences.

(j) **Assess mainstream vs. new/now (mass vs. networked.** In addition to traditional print and broadcast media, the Internet and satellite communications gives anyone with a cheap mobile phone the ability to move information and imagery to potentially millions of recipients via interconnected social networks.

(k) In any environment one of the quickest ways to establish a mass communication capability is by radio. Even in undeveloped areas, it is fairly economical to distribute low cost battery-powered radios to the population. Development and assistance NGOs in the joint operating area may agree to participate in radio distribution as they interact with the population.

"In Desert Storm PSYOP forces ran "Voice of the Gulf, "the Coalition's radio network that broadcast from ground based and airborne transmitters, 18 hours per day for 40 days. The radio script was prepared daily and provided news, countered Iraqi propaganda and disinformation, and encouraged Iraqi defection and surrender."

FINAL REPORT TO CONGRESS
CONDUCT OF THE PERSIAN GULF WAR
April 1992

(l) While working to rebuild mass media infrastructure the joint force can produce of flyers or handouts to disseminate information. In locations with low literacy rates, printed product distribution should focus on the local leadership who can share the information with those who cannot read. The requirement for the military to help rebuild or reestablish the infrastructure for newspaper operations is more likely than the need to actually run the paper itself Regardless of the medium being used, efforts should be made to work with local leaders and identify former news media professionals who can work with military media professionals to build the required capability. Viewers, listeners and readers should get their information from indigenous journalists as soon as feasible.

(m) **Components of Media Development**. The US Institute of Peace Stabilization and Reconstruction Series No. 7 breaks media development down into pre-deployment, deployment and exit phases. The tasks they associate with each phase follows and can be used by military planners to inform the role of the joint force in media development:

(n) **Business Development and Commercial Sustainability**. Even media outlets that survive a major conflict may not be able to sustain themselves on a commercial basis post conflict. JFCs may need to allocate resources to provide basic start-up or sustainment funding to get media outlets up and running[125].

(o) **Regulation**

1. A healthy media sector requires a credible and independent government regulatory body to establish licensing standards, monitor media abuses, and address complaints. Countries emerging from conflict frequently lack the framework of laws, regulations, and institutions necessary to regulate media outlets and ensure that the media is not subject to undue government or other outside influence.

2. JFCs should be prepared to support HN government efforts to create appropriate mechanisms to license and regulate media outlets while discouraging the adoption of regulatory mechanisms that would facilitate government or other outside interference with the freedom of the media. This may involve supporting efforts by the USG interagency or other partners to draft media legislation by funding expert domestic and/or foreign advisors to assist members of the national legislature.

f. Tasks Associated with Building Media

(1) **Essential tasks** are those tasks that may need to be undertaken in reconstruction and stabilization to support development of media in a post-conflict environment. Most of these tasks will be accomplished by civilian USG and other foreign donor government agencies, IGOs and other international organizations, and NGOs; but the joint force may need to support the effort if civilian agencies are limited by a hostile or uncertain security environment.[126] The essential tasks, relevant to building media, are summarized in Table IV-1 below.

(2) **Media development activities** the joint force or DOD may be particularly well-suited to support include the following:

(a) Establish Security

1. Provide security for key media facilities. This may include studios, transmission towers, and communication links for broadcast media and paper, printing presses, and central distribution facilities for print media. Task will continue until HN forces are able to assume role.

2. Provide security for local journalists in response to specific threats.

(b) **Support Restoration of Media Outlets**. Conduct emergency repairs of media infrastructure. This may include conducting emergency repair of broadcast and printing facilities needed for media outlets to resume operation as well as supporting supply of essential inputs such as electricity and newsprint.

(c) Support the Commercial Viability of Media Outlets

1. Provide content the media can use to fill pages or airtime tailored to meet the information needs of the readers/viewers/listeners

2. Provide technical assistance and training on the efficient operation of media outlets and commercially viable introduction of new communications technologies.

(d) Support Development of Journalism and Improvement in Media Quality

BUILDING MEDIA TASKS			
Growth Area	Initial Response	Transformation	Fostering Sustainability
Media Business Development	• Train media managers, advertising department staff, and business consultants • Provide small grants and low interest loans for start ups or rebuilding	• Develop in country business training and consulting capacity • Enhance know how of local businesses on how to use media ads effectively • Improve quality of audience research	• Develop viable media/ad markets • Assure even playing field by privatizing state media or converting them to public service media
Media Environment	• Develop regulatory environment for use of access to the media • Ensure appropriate balance between government and independent media • Support monitoring of media rights violations as well as of inflammatory or unprofessional media contents	• Provide media law training to lawyers, jurists, and media personnel • Build media rights advocacy groups • Pass and then enforce laws protecting the rights of the media	• Raise general citizen awareness of importance of independent media
Disseminate Information on Governance, Security, Humanitarian and Social Well-Being, Justice and Reconciliation, Economic Stabilization, and Infrastructure	• Identify or establish outlets for international, national, and local news media • Utilize media as public information tool to provide factual information and control rumors • Issue effective press releases and timely provision of information services as needed in local languages • Assist National Transitional Administration and/or National Government to inform public regularly	• Invest in the development of indigenous capacity • Train journalists, expand capacity of outlets and improve interaction with local population and linkages with the international community	

Table IV-1. Building Media Tasks

<u>1</u>. Provide training for journalists, editors, government spokesmen, and other media professionals.

<u>2</u>. Encourage media professionals to form journalist associations and adopt standards of professional conduct.

<u>3</u>. Encourage institutions for professional media education to add special training for conflict situations to their core curricula.

<u>4</u>. Support the upgrading of university journalism departments and the creation of journalism programs and internships with universities.

<u>5</u>. Support establishment of mid-career media training institutions to build the professional capacity of media workers.

<u>6</u>. Support mentoring programs that pair local media professionals with US and international counterparts.

(e) **Support Media Independence**. As appropriate to the environment, support the HN development of new media laws and regulations and, working with the legislative branch, support the elimination of unnecessary restrictions.

(f) **Liaison with Media Development**

<u>1</u>. Conduct a dialogue with government officials on the role of the media and the importance of a legal framework and policy environment that facilitates independent media operations.

<u>2</u>. Include content providers to the Internet and other new media in strategic communication and related outreach efforts.

<u>3</u>. Support the establishment or repair of Internet and other new media facilities.

<u>4</u>. Provide technical assistance and train content providers, such as radio and television stations and the print media, to incorporate Internet and other emerging media in their business models.

g. **Key Agencies and Stakeholders**. A range of organizations in the HN will have an interest in media development. While these groups will vary from country to country, host-nation partners will generally include universities, civil society, journalists unions and professional organizations, and political parties. In addition to collaborating with members of the US embassy and USAID in country, the JFC and staff should be cognizant of the following agencies and stakeholders.

(1) **Intergovernmental Organizations**

(a) The **International Program for the Development of Communication (IPDC)**, http://portal.unesco.org/ci/en/ev.php-URL ID=13270&URL DO=DO TOPIC &URL SECTION=201.html, is a forum established under the auspices of the UN Educational, Scientific, and Cultural Organization (UNESCO) that is intended to mobilize the international community to discuss and promote media development in developing countries. The IPDC is source of information and advice on media development and defense of press freedom. UNESCO's Communication and Information Sector, headquartered in Paris, oversees the IPDC.

(b) The **International Telecommunications Union (ITU)**, http://www.itu.int/ITU-D/ict/, is the leading UN agency for information and communication technology issues and the global focus point for governments and the private sector in developing networks and services. The ITU coordinates the shared global use of the radio spectrum, works to improve telecommunication infrastructure in the developing world, and establishes worldwide standards for the interconnection of communications systems. Headquartered in Geneva, the ITU is a source of information and data on global use of international communication technology.

(c) The **Organization for Economic Cooperation and Development (OECD)**, http://www.oecd.org/home/0,3305,en 2649 201185 1 1 1 1 1,00.html, promotes discussion on information and communication technologies (ICTs) in society and undertakes a range of activities aimed at improving international understanding of how ICTs contribute to sustainable economic growth and social well-being and their role in the shift toward knowledge-based societies. The OECD, headquartered in Paris, has a membership of 30 advanced developed countries.

(d) The **UNESCO Institute for Statistics**, http://stats.uis.unesco.org/nesco/tableviewer/document.aspx?ReportId=143, publishes statistics on newspapers and radio and television broadcasting worldwide.

(e) The **US Institute for Peace (USIP)**, http://www.usip.org, includes the Center of Innovation, an office that focuses on harnessing the power of the media for peace-building and developing strategies for countering the abuse of media during conflict. The center conducts research, develops programming across all forms of media, and promotes cooperation and information sharing among policymakers, experts, media actors, and peace-building practitioners.

(2) **Other National Development Agencies**. There are several other nations that have programs to support media development in post-conflict situations, generally through implementing partners. These include the UK's Department for International Development (DFID), the Canadian International Development Agency (CIDA), the Netherlands Ministry of Development Cooperation, Germany's Federal Ministry for Economic Cooperation and Development, Denmark's International Development Agency, Sweden's International Development Cooperation Agency (SIDA), the Norwegian Agency for Development Cooperation (NORAD), and several other major national development agencies. DOD personnel should contact the Office of the Secretary of Defense for Policy (OSD-P) to initiate contact with these agencies/

(3) **Nongovernmental Organizations and Implementing Partners**. Many organizations that are involved in media related issues are funded by private sources or have their own fund raising. Others are funded by USAID or other international development funding entities. The list below is illustrative, not definitive.

(a) The **International Research and Exchanges Board** (IREX), http://www.irex.org, develops independent media by working with local partners to advance the professionalism and long-term economic sustainability of newspapers, radio, television, and Internet media. IREX specialized programs and small grants build skills for balanced, investigative reporting, better media management, and advocacy for press freedoms. Program areas include journalism training and education, media strategy and management, business development and advertising, news and public affairs production, media law reform and advocacy, and technology and infrastructure development.

(b) The **Internews Network**, http://www.internews.org/default.shtm, is an international media development organization whose mission is to empower local media worldwide. Headquartered in California, the Internews Network has offices in 35 countries in Asia, Europe, the Middle East, and North America and is a founding member of Internews International, an umbrella organization, based in Paris, made up of 12 media development NGOs. Internews activities include providing training in journalism; media production and management, including computer graphics, media law, and investigative journalism; programming production; and media infrastructure. Internews also assists media outlets, providing journalists and stations with production equipment, creating production studios and building radio stations from the ground up, and provides training on media law and policy.

(c) The **Institute for War and Peace Reporting (IWPR)**, http://iwpr.net, trains journalists and works with local media in areas of conflict, with the aim of building democratic societies. IWPR has an international network for media development that supports training and capacity-building programs for local journalism in over two dozen countries. It sometimes works as an implementing agency for the UK's DFID as well as other international development agencies

(d) **America's Development Foundation (ADF)**, http://www.adfusa.org, implements a wide range of development programs, including programs for developing independent media, in countries undergoing a transition to democracy. It works on building media capacity to provide independent and balanced coverage of news and public affairs via television, radio and print media and provides professional training for journalists, media business managers and others. It also has programs to establish the necessary regulatory and policy environment to support an independent media. ADF has programs in over 30 countries.

(e) The mission of **Search for Common Ground**, http://www.sfcg.org, is "to transform the way the world deals with conflict away from adversarial approaches, towards cooperative solutions." Part of its "toolkit" includes development of radio and television studios that produce news, features, drama, and music. It also trains journalists, emphasizing the importance of diminish inflammatory reporting and promoting mutual understanding. It has seventeen field programs on four continents, operates a news service in the Middle East, and produces magazines in the Balkans.

(f) The **National Democratic Institute for International Affairs (NDI)**, http://www.ndi.org, and the **International Republican Institute (IRI)**, http://www.iri.org, provide practical assistance to civic and political leaders worldwide to advance democratic values, practices and institutions and build civil society. While NDI and IRI do not engage in media development as a primary task, they do some media-related work, for example with media as it is related to elections, citizen participation in governance, political parties, and constituent communications.

(g) Deutsche-Welle (DW), http://dw-world.de/dw, runs the DW-AKADEMIE, where radio professionals from developing and transition countries can receive training. The DW-AKADEMIE's goal is the promotion of freedom of opinion around the world through projects that contribute to more openness, transparency and participation in the electronic media of developing and transition countries. It works on location in Africa, Asia, Latin America, Europe and Central Asia, and the Middle East. The majority of its funding comes from the German Ministry for Economic Cooperation and Development. The DW-AKADEMIE also works with the German Foreign Ministry, the European Union, and the World Bank.

(h) The **BBC World Service Trust**, http://www.bbc.co.uk/worldservice/ trust, is the BBC's international charity. Its mission is to use media and communications to reduce poverty and promote human rights internationally. One of the Trust's primary objectives is to strengthen the media sector in developing countries by providing training to all types of media professionals and media outlets, as well as technical support and infrastructure. It delivers training and management programs in Asia, Africa, the Middle East, Latin America, and Europe. The Trust works with governments, broadcasters, media professionals, and civil society institutions in developing and transitional countries and also partners with UN agencies and NGOs.

(i) Established in 1985, **Reporters without Borders**, http://www.rsf.com, works to publicize and **defend** journalists and media personnel imprisoned or mistreated for doing their work, campaigns against censorship and laws that undermine press freedom, and provides **financial aid** to journalists or media outlets in difficulty (to pay for lawyers, medical care and equipment) as well to the families of imprisoned journalists. The group also works to improve the safety of journalists, particularly those reporting in war zones. The organization, which is registered in France as **Reporters sans frontières** (RSF), is present on five continents and has consultant status at the United Nations.

Intentionally Blank

APPENDIX A
MILITARY TASKS FOR SUPPORT TO POST-CONFLICT GOVERNANCE

GOVERNANCE	TASKS	PLANNING CONSIDERATIONS
Constitutional Processes	➢ Establish liaison with Embassy political section and USAID DG officer. ➢ Provide legal expertise, as requested, especially on the security sector. ➢ Provide security, in support of local forces, for drafters' meeting sites, for public fora and during a referendum. ➢ Provide logistics support as required.	➢ The military role will likely be focused on logistics, security and the provision of legal expertise. ➢ The military may also play a constructive role by ensuring US and international agencies address defense/security affairs and include mechanisms for civilian oversight. ➢ Basic rules governing the constitution development process should be established at the outset and should engage the public. ➢ Strengthening the legislature as a check on excessive executive power should be a factor in constitutional development. ➢ Public participation in constitutional development requires social inclusion, personal security, and freedom of speech and assembly.
National Governance: *Initial or "First-Response"*	➢ Determine the need for first response governance to address a leadership vacuum. ➢ Identify and prioritize unmet institutional needs for government services. ➢ Protect key government leaders, ministry buildings, and other facilities. ➢ Conduct emergency repairs to key government buildings and facilities.	➢ Military forces should anticipate the possibility of conducting a broad range of governance activities that are normally handled by civilians. ➢ It is desirable for military planners to conduct or have available a predeployment governance assessment prepared in coordination with or by civilian agencies to determine the likely condition and needs of the mission area. ➢ Embedding governance advisors in the military force structure prior to deployment enables them to accompany forces and provide advice on critical first response governance decisions. ➢ Restoring basic public services disrupted by conflict should have high priority. ➢ It should be anticipated that JTF commanders will need funds both to support HN establishment of ministries and other key government institutions quickly and to facilitate payment of essential civil service workers such as teachers, police, medical personnel, and administrators. ➢ The terms of international mandates and peace agreements that affect post-conflict governance should be available to planners so they can be incorporated in the planning process.

Table A-1. Military Tasks for Support to Post-Conflict Governance

GOVERNANCE	TASKS	PLANNING CONSIDERATIONS
National Governance: *Transition*	➢ Support establishment of transitional political authority, if necessary by helping to identify and select leaders for an interim or transitional government. ➢ Participate in senior-level discussions on the establishment of an interim or transitional national government. ➢ Participate in the vetting of proposed appointees to interim or transitional government positions. ➢ Provide strategic communications support to the transitional government. ➢ Provide logistics support to key national-level leaders.	➢ Holding personnel changes in the government bureaucracy to a minimum can help avoid disruptions in the delivery of government services ➢ Finding ways to limit purely political appointments to government positions can help ensure they are filled by technically qualified persons. ➢ International civilian plans to assist national governance structures can change over time and should be monitored continuously by planners. ➢ Transparent and accountable budget processes are important in both military and HN government programs that generate or manage revenue. ➢ Establish advisory councils and other mechanisms for citizen input as early as possible. ➢ Don't make personnel decisions that aggravate the conflict.
Local Governance: *First-Response*	➢ Provide first response governance to deliver essential and critical government services. ➢ Identify and establish early contact with government leaders at the provincial and local levels. ➢ Begin communicating immediately with the local populace. ➢ Protect provincial and local government leaders and facilities.	➢ If resources are limited, it may be necessary to prioritize governance assistance programs. ➢ One solution to resource limitations is to work directly with a limited number of local governments on a pilot basis, then disseminate Information on innovations and replicate successful activities in other localities at a later time. ➢ If the former government exercised strong centralized control over the country, it may be necessary to work with the national legislature to pass laws that give local governments more authority and access to revenue than they previously enjoyed. ➢ Since government authority may need to be decentralized in some countries but centralized in others, planners should be aware of USG policies regarding to the need to promote centralization/ decentralization in the Host Nation. ➢ Encouraging the establishment of civic and professional associations can help generate and focus citizen input on legislative proposals that affect local government.

Table A-1. Military Tasks for Support to Post-Conflict Governance (Cont)

GOVERNANCE	TASKS	PLANNING CONSIDERATIONS
Local Governance: *Transitional*	➤ Provide support to interim provincial and local government leaders. ➤ Participate in vetting proposed appointees to provincial and local government positions. ➤ Provide strategic communications support to provincial and local governments. ➤ Support establishment of a liaison process between local and national-level government authorities and institutions. ➤ Support priority local government operations and provision of services. ➤ Build the capacity of provincial and local authorities to deliver government services.	➤ Local and provincial governments should be encouraged to adopt procedures that give citizens a voice on security sector reform and other major local government decisions ➤ Assistance program managers should elicit and incorporate citizen input in decisions on assisting local governance. ➤ Local and provincial government officials should be encouraged to build skills in strategic and financial planning. ➤ Improvements and innovations in local governance can be leveraged to have an impact at the national level by widely publicized them throughout the country. ➤ Nontraditional groups such as women, ethnic groups, and other minorities should be actively encouraged to participate in local government.
Legislative Strengthening	➤ Establish contact and work closely with the Embassy political section and USAID's DG officers. ➤ Make sure US and other programs supporting legislative strengthening plan for the legislature's role in defense and security affairs. ➤ Advise US civilian agencies, if needed, on ways for the new legislature to strengthen its role in security sector oversight (*e.g.* formation and role of defense and intelligence committees, defense budget procedures). ➤ Assist with development of infrastructure, facilities, equipment, and material needs of the new legislature, as requested. ➤ Advise local forces on security procedures and arrangements for the new legislature's facilities and members.	➤ The military's role is likely to be focused primarily on logistics and security. ➤ Working with a parliamentary system will be different than working with a presidential system.

Table A-1. Military Tasks for Support to Post-Conflict Governance (Cont)

GOVERNANCE	TASKS	PLANNING CONSIDERATIONS
Political Parties	➤ Establish liaison with Embassy political officers and USAID DG officers. ➤ Assess existing political parties and political leadership and provide assessments to Embassy political and USAID DG officers. ➤ Share information with USG civilian agencies on political leaders who have links with militias or paramilitary forces. ➤ Provide information to HN groups seeking US support on US policy in support of democratic political party development. ➤ Provide security, with HN security forces, and support for meetings between various social groups and/or political parties. ➤ Identify needs of US and other programs and determine ways in which military support might supplement their programs (*e.g.* assistance in printing party materials, media support). ➤ Provide logistics support, such as transportation, for political party poll watchers and monitors when elections are held. (See the section of this handbook on elections.)	➤ The military's role in political party development is likely to be limited. ➤ Avoid giving the impression of favoritism in contacts with political party leadership. ➤ USAID, UNDP and other donors are potential sources of training and support to parties that meet international criteria. ➤ The most valuable contribution to political party development will probably be the overall maintenance of security so that parties may engage in peaceful competition. ➤ There should be no US military footprint on political party development.

Table A-1. Military Tasks for Support to Post-Conflict Governance (Cont)

GOVERNANCE	TASKS	PLANNING CONSIDERATIONS
Civil Society	➤ Begin interacting with civil society organizations as early as possible. ➤ Provide logistical support to key civil society leaders to facilitate their participation in public discussions involving the government and citizens. ➤ Encourage host country leaders to engage and seek the views of civil society as new laws and government structures are established. ➤ Support civil society efforts to deliver public services and conduct public information campaigns. ➤ Provide technical assistance and training to civil society organizations on subjects related to their operations.	➤ Building civil society requires understanding the cultural and historical context of the country. ➤ Don't sidetrack deliberative public discussion in order to expedite policy change. ➤ Encourage intergroup partnerships and community-building functions at the local level and link these efforts to national governance initiatives. ➤ Raise the public visibility and status of civil society organizations by including them in public policy discussions and outreach efforts as well as in public service projects conducted by military forces. ➤ Include evaluation of laws governing NGOs and civil society in any assessment of HN laws and regulations by a military JAG. ➤ Encourage civil society groups to create or strengthen umbrella organizations that can represent their views to the national government.
Political Reconciliation		➤ Sponsoring and supporting political dialogue between representatives of opposing groups and communities can promote reconciliation. ➤ When there are deep communal divisions, creating opportunities for intergroup collaborative projects can promote reconciliation at a local level. ➤ In many cases reconciliation means building relationships between social and ethnic groups that did not exist prior to the conflict. ➤ Social and political dimensions of interactions between US armed forces and the local population can unintentionally exacerbate tensions or rivalries. ➤ A difficult dilemma found in some post-conflict situations involves the tradeoff between restoring a sense of justice and setting aside the prosecution of past abuses in the interests of maintaining social and political stability.

Table A-1. Military Tasks for Support to Post-Conflict Governance (Cont)

GOVERNANCE	TASKS	PLANNING CONSIDERATIONS
Anti-Corruption	(Direct tasking is unlikely; any tasks will usually be residual or assigned by USG civilian leadership. However, there may be direct tasks in the context of mil-mil relationships).	➢ It is important to avoid raising unrealistic expectations. Overly ambitious anti-corruption promises that cannot be implemented risk undermining the credibility and legitimacy of international donors and local leaders.
		➢ The role of military forces in anti-corruption efforts may vary depending on conditions. In a hostile or uncertain environment, the military may lead reform. When nonmilitary agencies are present, the security situation may still require extensive military support to civilian programs. When the security situation permits more normal civilian programs, the military role is usually limited to the HN defense sector.
		➢ Checks and balances are critical elements in preventing corruption, even though they may slow down rebuilding efforts.
		➢ Electoral politics usually increase the importance of money in politics, multiplying the incentives for corruption.
		➢ The pressure and chaos of an emergency can result in neglecting recordkeeping and competitive procurement rules. In the longer term, these same problems can occur if weak government institutions are overwhelmed with assistance. It is important to be aware of absorptive capacity.
		➢ Potential sources of corruption in the defense sector are defense officials (ministerial and military staff); defense institutions (ministries and armed forces); and political context and controls.
		➢ Areas for training include prevention of military procurement fraud and professional audit and control standards (including the defense budget).
		➢ If HN is party to international treaties and conventions on anti-corruption, advisors may be able to use this to justify stronger anti-corruption efforts within the armed forces and defense/security ministries.
		➢ The long-term costs of including corrupt elites as part of a post-conflict government should be balanced against the need for post-conflict stability.

Table A-1. Military Tasks for Support to Post-Conflict Governance (Cont)

GOVERNANCE	TASKS	PLANNING CONSIDERATIONS
Governance, SSR & SFA	(Refer to JFC Handbook for Rule of Law and Security Sector Reform)	➢ It is difficult to set comprehensive SSR objectives in the early stages of a transition from war to peace because of political machinations and inadequate capacity. The latter stages of the transition may offer a better opportunity. ➢ A sequencing problem can develop if strengthening security sector bodies is given more emphasis than building capacity for rule of law, justice, and democratic governance. Sequencing is also a problem when international assistance programs move forward before the HN has identified its priorities. ➢ Short-term force generation requirements should be balanced against adherence to longer-term SSR principles to avoid creating an overly militarized society. ➢ Legislative and judicial oversight of the security sector is essential for effective governance. Appropriate checks and balances can help prevent the executive from dominating through intimidation ➢ Reconstituted security forces, especially the national army, should be firmly under the control and management of the newly established civilian government. Use of militias may provide short-term stability but lead to longer-term problems if they refuse to disarm or to integrate with government security forces. ➢ A critical focus of SSR is the bureaucratic agency responsible for the police and other internal security forces, usually the Ministry of Interior. Often international donors go straight to training police, with little attention to the interior ministry to which the police report. ➢ It is difficult to find qualified civilian leaders and staff to manage and oversee the security sector in many post-conflict countries. Appointment of local power brokers may help keep the peace and reduce crime, but can also undermine legitimacy of new security institutions. ➢ Advisors in security ministries should not merely be experts but should be negotiators, teachers and partners. The characteristics of successful advisors differ from those required to actually execute the task for which they are advising, particularly in the military context. ➢ Delivering justice, while at the same time preserving stability in a post-conflict society, requires maintaining a delicate balance.

Table A-1. Military Tasks for Support to Post-Conflict Governance (Cont)

Intentionally Blank

APPENDIX B
PRINCIPLES AND TASKS FOR MILITARY SUPPORT TO POST-CONFLICT ELECTIONS

1. Principles

While there are no standardized principles for military support to elections, the following principles could be applied:

a. Unity of effort.

b. Support a HN process and promote ownership.

c. Maintain political neutrality.

d. Build confidence in election security.

e. Develop HN capacity.

f. Enable stability.

g. Expand partnerships.

h. Plan for post-election follow-through.

i. Embed elections into a larger governance and conflict transformation strategy.

2. Election Operations Support

ELECTION OPERATIONS	KEY MILITARY TASKS	PLANNING CONSIDERATIONS AND NOTES
	ALL ELECTION PHASES	
	Security ➢ Deter and defeat threats. ➢ Rebuild, reform, and expand indigenous security forces. ➢ Coordinate and integrate security operations with HN security forces and election officials. ➢ Secure key election facilities, teaming with HN security forces, if capable and available. **Public Information and Civic Education** ➢ Perform public affairs and outreach in coordination with US Embassy and election authority. **Intelligence and Information-Gathering** ➢ Provide J2 intelligence on threats to elections to HN, JIIM partners, and other relevant participants. ➢	➢ Planners should take into account the cultural context of the election, taking steps that may be necessary to maximize participation of women and any other traditionally marginalized groups. ➢ The JTF should work with the US embassy to ensure that threat information is shared with civilian donors, international organizations, and nongovernmental organizations supporting the elections. ➢ Key coordination areas for military are Security, Public Affairs, and Civic Outreach.

Table B-1. Election Operations Support

ELECTION OPERATIONS	KEY MILITARY TASKS	PLANNING CONSIDERATIONS AND NOTES
PRE-ELECTION PERIOD		
	Stakeholder Coordination ➢ Participate in principals, donors, implementing agencies coordination fora.	
Legal Framework, Electoral Regulations & Complaint Commissions ➢ Legal Basis for Elections established. ➢ Legal Framework established. ➢ Development and Issuance of Electoral Regulations.	➢ Analyze peace agreement/UN resolution for guidance & requirements. ➢ Assess needs for legal reform. ➢ Provide legal expertise to election law drafting committee. ➢ Facilitate security and logistics planning for major public events. ➢ Secure government officials and facilities involved in developing the legal framework/constitution. ➢ Provide logistics support for key events. ➢ Provide election experts, generally JAG and Civil Affairs, to electoral legal working groups if needed.	➢ Establishment of an election complaints and appeals unit is critical. It links citizens to the election process; provides legal recourse for complaints, reduces the possibility of violent conflict, and increases the legitimacy of the electoral process. However, the legal framework is usually new and will be severely tested in the complaints process. It is imperative to have attorneys from a variety of traditions work together in establishing process, regulations and decisions. For a credible complaints and appeals process, it is vital to recruit & train investigators.
Operational Planning	➢ Provide planners to assist the election authority. ➢ Develop Mil Election Support Plan that includes Security, Public Affairs, Civic Outreach, Logistics, Communications & Civilian Coordination sub-plans. ➢ Establish military liaisons to US EMB, UN, election teams & relevant working groups (security, public affairs, outreach, logistics). ➢ Coordinate w/ election authority in security plan development. ➢ Establish joint planning groups that include all relevant ministries. ➢ Plan for election operations center (joint elections security center may be co-located). ➢ Plan use of, and work with, private security contractors - ops/log./sec/medical .support. ➢ Prepare budget & funding requests. ➢ Assess threats and anticipate actions to disrupt elections.	➢ An interagency, multilateral cooperation plan is usually overlooked, but is important. ➢ Liaison requirements may be extensive. There are typically multiple strategic, operational and tactical election working groups. These may include the HN election commission and ministries of defense and interior, the US EMB, the UN, and other military forces. In addition to organizational liaisons, there will also be functional working groups (security, public affairs, outreach, and donor coordination) to which military liaisons should be appointed. ➢ An election period will usually require additional military forces. ➢ Planning for rotations during this period should include time for new arrivals to receive adequate orientation on election tasks. ➢ Military assets such as air and land transportation are often called upon for an election. ➢ Plan for special needs & external voters (military, IDPs, nomads, citizens returning from overseas).

Table B-1. Election Operations Support (Cont)

ELECTION OPERATIONS	KEY MILITARY TASKS	PLANNING CONSIDERATIONS AND NOTES
PRE-ELECTION PERIOD (CONT'D)		
Security Concept of Operations ➢ Establishment of safe and secure environment for the conduct of election campaign, voting, counting ballots, announcement of results, political transitions, and inauguration of new office holders.	➢ Conduct an election security assessment. ➢ Coordinate planning and operations for security. ➢ Participate/establish HN national, sub national/provincial, and local/municipal security groups. ➢ Establish and staff joint election security operations group. ➢ Establish or ensure lines of communication are at all levels, from the operations center down to individual polling places. ➢ Prepare daily election threat analyses. ➢ Identify election security "hot spots" or "watch areas." ➢ Plan for protection of election workers, election materials, registration, observers, voting sites & counting sites. ➢ Organize training & rehearsals for security operations. ➢ Ensure safe movement of media personnel during election season. ➢ Ensure security for ballots during printing & pre election storage. ➢ Conduct security briefings for international observers. ➢ Develop emergency & evacuation procedures for observers & identify "no go" areas. ➢ Plan for crowd control & potential disturbances at polls. ➢ Secure voted ballots while results are being validated.	➢ Private contractors are increasingly being used during post conflict elections to provide security for facilities and candidates, and more importantly to provide field operational linkages between election authorities and international military forces. ➢ Consider geographic phasing of voter registration so security resources can be concentrated if HN security forces are not to full capacity "rolling elections." ➢ It is critical that ballots are secured before and after the voting; otherwise allegations of ballot duplication and fraud can undermine the election's legitimacy and credibility.

Table B-1. Election Operations Support (Cont)

ELECTION OPERATIONS	KEY MILITARY TASKS	PLANNING CONSIDERATIONS AND NOTES
PRE-ELECTION PERIOD (CONT'D)		
Voter Registration ➢ Voters registered.	➢ Develop Concept of Operations. ➢ Synchronize security operations with registration efforts. ➢ Provide logistical and security support to possibly thousands of voter registration sites and to mobile registration teams. ➢ Assist registration teams in gaining access to remote or high threat areas. ➢ Monitor voter registration mobile teams and registration of nomad, armed forces, IDPs, & refugees.	➢ In most post conflict elections, voter registration cards are needed and become a powerful symbol of a country's new beginning. Older ID and citizenship records may have been destroyed in the conflict, or were issued by a discredited former government. ➢ Voter registration can serve as a temporary substitute for a census. Conducting a new census is always controversial in a conflict zone because of implications about ethnic/religious status and rights of citizenship. ➢ Duplicating and selling voter cards becomes a primary concern during elections. Technological advances will eventually limit voter card fraud by embedding non transferrable, non duplicating information. ➢ Demining may be necessary at voter registration sites in areas that have been in conflict for decades.
Host Nation Security Force Training & Mentoring ➢ Host Nation able to provide security needed for elections.	➢ Develop a plan for building the capacity of security forces (police & military). ➢ Provide election specific training for security forces (principles or best practices, public affairs, election operations, security, etc). ➢ Assist security forces (police and military) with establishing transparent and accountable rules for procurement of commodities. ➢ Conduct Rapid Action training. ➢ Train police for crowd control. ➢ Prepare security forces to assist in logistics planning & movement of materials. ➢ Plan for post election evaluation of security forces.	➢ Elections are an excellent opportunity for security force capacity building and capability development. ➢ Any security force development should be part of a broader plan for governance strengthening and HN institutional development, at both the national (interior and defense ministries) and local levels. ➢ In a first post conflict election, US military forces often have to provide security and communications equipment, vehicles, and other commodities for the conduct a safe election. Plan on deficiencies and be prepared to provide equipment as necessary. ➢ Plan for post election security reform as needed.

Table B-1. Election Operations Support (Cont)

GOVERNANCE	TASKS	PLANNING CONSIDERATIONS
Civil Society	➢ Begin interacting with civil society organizations as early as possible. ➢ Provide logistical support to key civil society leaders to facilitate their participation in public discussions involving the government and citizens. ➢ Encourage host country leaders to engage and seek the views of civil society as new laws and government structures are established. ➢ Support civil society efforts to deliver public services and conduct public information campaigns. ➢ Provide technical assistance and training to civil society organizations on subjects related to their operations.	➢ Building civil society requires understanding the cultural and historical context of the country. ➢ Don't sidetrack deliberative public discussion in order to expedite policy change. ➢ Encourage intergroup partnerships and community-building functions at the local level and link these efforts to national governance initiatives. ➢ Raise the public visibility and status of civil society organizations by including them in public policy discussions and outreach efforts as well as in public service projects conducted by military forces. ➢ Include evaluation of laws governing NGOs and civil society in any assessment of HN laws and regulations by a military JAG. ➢ Encourage civil society groups to create or strengthen umbrella organizations that can represent their views to the national government.
Political Reconciliation		➢ Sponsoring and supporting political dialogue between representatives of opposing groups and communities can promote reconciliation. ➢ When there are deep communal divisions, creating opportunities for intergroup collaborative projects can promote reconciliation at a local level. ➢ In many cases reconciliation means building relationships between social and ethnic groups that did not exist prior to the conflict. ➢ Social and political dimensions of interactions between US armed forces and the local population can unintentionally exacerbate tensions or rivalries. ➢ A difficult dilemma found in some post-conflict situations involves the tradeoff between restoring a sense of justice and setting aside the prosecution of past abuses in the interests of maintaining social and political stability.

Table B-1. Election Operations Support (Cont)

ELECTION OPERATIONS	KEY MILITARY TASKS	PLANNING CONSIDERATIONS AND NOTES
ELECTION PERIOD		
Public Affairs/Communication ➢ Candidates communicate their platforms and policies. ➢ Citizens and candidates are informed about election deadlines, regulations, requirements and encouraged to participate.	➢ Rebuild critical media infrastructure for election communication. ➢ Identify, establish, and protect (as needed) outlets for news media. ➢ Participate in public affairs coordination group to improve public messaging and leverage communication assets. ➢ Issue press releases supporting election authority's daily talking points. ➢ Provide public outreach messaging, in support of election authority's PA effort. ➢ Develop provincial/regional public messaging with HN. ➢ Coordinate with election authority and donors to establish election media center. ➢ Provide training/mentoring to journalists & media professionals as needed. ➢ Control for misinformation and disinformation. ➢ Monitor public opinion. ➢ Support development of HN security forces' public affairs capabilities.	
Civic Outreach & Information ➢ Civic Education campaign conducted. ➢ Citizens and candidates informed about election deadlines, regulations, requirements and encouraged to participate.	➢ Develop election education outreach for HN security forces and civilian audiences. ➢ Provide logistics to support civic outreach and public information. ➢ Provide poster, radios, radio stations, and other military communication assets for election authority if needed. ➢ Assist in distribution of voter education materials If needed. ➢ Protect mobile voter education & outreach workers. ➢ Provide security for media outlets.	

Table B-1. Election Operations Support (Cont)

ELECTION OPERATIONS	KEY MILITARY TASKS	PLANNING CONSIDERATIONS AND NOTES
ELECTION PERIOD (CONT'D)		
Distribution of Election Materials ➢ Sensitive & non sensitive election materials distributed.	➢ Secure distribution of sensitive election materials. ➢ Support election logistics efforts as required. ➢ Secure ballots before/after voting; during storage, transportation, collection, and counting. ➢ Escort ballots & boxes in transit in presence of observers.	➢ Large money contracts for activities such as printing ballots and transportation are ripe for fraud, graft and corruption. Developing anti corruption measures is necessary. ➢ If ballots are not secured before/after voting, ballot duplication and fraud can undermine election's legitimacy and credibility. ➢ If US/International forces assist in the transportation of ballots, it is crucial that election observers accompany ballots to guard against accusations of military/international ballot tampering.
Election Observation, Monitoring and Supervision ➢ Elections are internationally validated and international standards accepted by HN.	➢ Develop emergency & evacuation procedures for observers & identify "no go" areas. ➢ Meet with stakeholders, donors, and other observation patrons. ➢ Develop security plans for transport of possibly thousands of observers and/or work with private security companies and HN security forces for the safe movement of observers.	➢ In a high profile election, thousands of international election observers may arrive days before the voting. At a minimum, they will request meetings with US and military forces, desire security briefings and may presume that international military forces will provide personal security for their delegations. Observer groups often represent a country or governmental organization and will expect their troops to assist.
Conduct of Voting ➢ Ballots cast. ➢ Political party observers present at polling sites.	➢ Conduct area security in key population centers and along lines of communication. ➢ Establish quick reaction forces with coverage of key population centers.	

Table B-1. Election Operations Support (Cont)

ELECTION OPERATIONS	KEY MILITARY TASKS	PLANNING CONSIDERATIONS AND NOTES
POST-ELECTION PERIOD		
Counting and Collection of Ballots	➢ Protect counting centers. ➢ Transport and secure ballot boxes and election materials as necessary. ➢ Provide security and storage/archiving for voted ballots and other election materials.	➢ When Joint Forces are involved in securing or transporting election materials, those materials should be handled only by authorized election officials, if possible with independent observers present.
Announcement of Results/Elected Officials Take Office.	➢ Be prepared to respond to reactions by election losers. ➢ Protect inauguration events as necessary.	➢ Election security needs do not end on voting day. Post election presents several security challenges. Counting, the announcement of winners and losers, and the inauguration of new political leaders are prime disruption opportunities.
Evaluation and After-Action reviews	➢ Organize and conduct after action evaluations and gather "lessons learned."	Since international observer missions depart a country quickly after an election, planners should anticipate that any interviews of observers be conducted quickly once observation is finished.

Table B-1. Election Operations Support (Cont)

APPENDIX C
COMPARING ASSESSMENT FRAMEWORKS

Type	Assessment Agent	Scope	Purpose	Geographical coverage	Methodology	Selected Examples (Reference)
1. Governance Assessments	Government aid agencies	Electoral democracy, accountable government, the rule of law	Means to select and monitor aid projects	New democracies	Country-specific assessments against agency-derived indicators	CIDA (1) DFID (2) USAID (3) EU (4) Millennium Challenge Account (5) APRM (6)
2. Democracy Indices	Social and political scientists	Civil and political rights, electoral democracy	Explore empirical relationships between democracy and other variables (e.g. economic development and conflict)	Some global, some new democracies	Aggregate quantitative indicators (dichotomous or polychotomous)	Lipset (7) Diamond (8) Hadenius (9) M Moore (10) Kaufman et al. (11) Przeworski et al. (12) Polity IV (13) Bertelsmann Transformation Index (14) EIU (15)
3. International IDEA Democracy Assessment	National and international civil society, and governments	Full range of political and social democracy	Enhance public debate; identify & evaluate reform priorities	Global	Country-specific qualitative assessments by in-country experts	Transparency International (16) International IDEA-sponsored
4. Democratic Audits	Joint civil society initiatives	Civil and political rights, electoral democracy, accountable government	Raising consciousness about democracy and its condition	Old democracies	Country-specific qualitative assessment by citizens	Canada (17) Sweden (18) UK (19) Australia (20) Denmark (21) Netherlands (22) EU (23)
5. Economic and Social Assessments	International agencies and governments	Economic and social indicators	Guide to externally funded economic and social investment	Global	Quantitative indicators to assess comparative performance	UNDP (24) World Bank (25) Social Watch (26)
6. Human Rights Surveys	International NGOs and governments	Civil and political rights; economic social and cultural rights	Civil and political rights; economic social and cultural rights	Global	Quantitative or qualitative comparison between countries	Freedom House (27) Humana Index (28) Human Rights Watch (29) Amnesty International (30) US State Dept (31) CIRI Human Rights DataProject (32)

Table C-1. Comparing Assessment Frameworks

REFERENCES

1. Kapoor, I. (for Canadian International Development Agency, CIDA), *Indicators for Programming in Human Rights and Democratic Development: A Preliminary Study* (Ottawa: CIDA, 1996); CIDA, 'CIDA's Framework for Assessing Gender Equality Results', 2005.

2. UK Department for International Development (DFID), *Participatory Governance Assessment Framework: Improving the Quality of Governance to Help Eliminate Poverty* (London: DFID, 2002).

3. United States Agency for International Development (USAID), *Handbook of Democracy and Governance Program Indicators* (Washington, DC: USAID, 1998).

4. European Commission, *Regular Report from the Commission on Progress towards Accession by Each of the Candidate Countries* (Brussels: European Commission, annual).

5. 'Millennium Challenge Account: A New Compact for Global Development', *Economic Perspectives: An Electronic Journal of the US Department of State*, 8/2 (March 2003), available at <http://usinfo.state.gov/journals/ites/0303/ijee/ijee0303.htm>. For further information, see <http://www.mca.gov/index.php>.

6. New Partnership for Africa's Development (NEPAD), *African Peer Review Mechanism*, <http://www.nepad.org/aprm/>.

7. Lipset, S. M., 'Some Social Requisites of Democracy', *American Journal of Political Science*, 53 (1959).

8. Diamond, L., 'Economic Development and Democracy Reconsidered', *American Behavioral Scientist*, 35/4–5 (1992), pp. 450–99.

9. Hadenius, A., *Democracy and Development* (Cambridge: Cambridge University Press, 1992).

10. Moore, M., 'Democracy and Development in Cross-national Perspective: A New Look at the Statistics', *Democratisation*, 2/2 (1995).

11. Kaufman, D., Kraay, A. and Mastruzzi, M., *Governance Matters V: Aggregate and Individual Governance Indicators for 1996–2005*, Policy Research Working Paper (Washington, DC: World Bank, 2006).

12. Przeworski, A., Alvarez, M., Cheibub, J. A. and Limongi, F., *Democracy and Development: Political Institutions and Well Being in the World, 1950–1990*, Cambridge Studies in the Theory of Democracy no. 3 (Cambridge: Cambridge Assessing the Quality of Democracy: A Practical Guide 308 University Press, 2000). Data sets available at <http://www.ssc.upenn.edu/~cheibub/data/Default.htm>.

13. 'Political Regime Characteristics and Transitions, 1800–2004', Polity IV Project. Data sets and publications available at <http://www.cidcm.umd.edu/polity/>.

14. Bertelsmann Foundation (eds), *Bertelsmann Transformation Index 2003: Towards Democracy and a Market Economy* (Gütersloh: Bertelsmann Foundation, 2005). Datasets available at <http://www.bertelsmann-transformation-index.de/11.0.html?&L=1>.

15. 'The Economist Intelligence Unit's Index of Democracy', *The World in 2007*, available at <http://www.eiu.com/>.

16. Pope, J. (for Transparency International), *TI Source Book 2000 Confronting Corruption: The Elements of a National Integrity System* (Berlin: Transparency

International, 2000).

17. *The Canadian Democratic Audit Series*, USB Press, since 2004.

18. Centre for Business and Policy Studies (Studieförbundet näringsliv och samhälle, SNS), *Democratic Audit of Sweden* (Uppsala: Uppsala University, annually since 1995)

19. Klug, Francesca, Starmer, Keir and Weir, Stuart, *The Three Pillars of Liberty: Political Rights and Freedoms in the United Kingdom* (London: Routledge, 1996); and Beetham, David, Byrne, Iain, Ngan, Pauline and Weir, Stuart, *Democracy under Blair: A Democratic Audit of the United Kingdom*, 2nd ed (London: Politico's, 2002).

20. Democratic Audit of Australia, *Australia: State of Democracy* (forthcoming, 2008).

21. Danish Association for International Cooperation (Mellemfolkeligt Samvirke, MS) Democracy Audit, <http://www.ms.dk/sw47132.asp>.

22. Netherlands Ministry of the Interior and Kingdom Relations, *The State of Our Democracy 2006* (provisional translation), <http://www.minbzk.nl/bzk2006uk/>.

23. Lord, Christopher, *A Democratic Audit of the European Union* (Basingstoke: Palgrave Macmillan, 2004).

24. United Nations Development Programme (UNDP), *Human Development Report 2005* (Oxford: Oxford University Press, 2005).

25. World Bank, *World Development Indicators 2006* (Washington, DC: World Bank, 2006); World Bank Country Performance and Institutional Assessment (CPIA) framework, available at <http://www.worldbank.org>.

26. Social Watch (country and thematic reports published on an ongoing basis).

27. Freedom House, *Freedom in the World: The Annual Survey of Political Rights and Civil Liberties 2005* (Washington, DC: Freedom House, 2006).

28. Humana, C., *World Human Rights Guide* (Oxford: Oxford University Press, 1992).

29. Human Rights Watch, *Human Rights Watch World Report 2006* (New York: Human Rights Watch, 2006).

30. Amnesty International, *Amnesty International Report 2006: The State of the World's Human Rights* (London: Amnesty International, 2006).

31. US State Department, *2005 Country Reports on Human Rights Practices* (Washington, DC: US Government Printing Office, 2006).

32. Cingranelli-Richards (CIRI) Human Rights Data Project, <http://www.humanrightsdata.org>.

Intentionally Blank

APPENDIX D
REFERENCES AND WEB SITES FOR KEY STAKEHOLDERS, DONORS, AND IMPLEMENTING PARTNERS

1. Introduction

Governance and elections are vitally important in post-conflict planning, stabilization, and reconstruction. Both the USG and allied governments around the world have come to recognize their importance and a proliferation of materials, books, publications, and news articles, are now available in many languages. The list of references offered here is not intended to be either exhaustive or comprehensive. We have endeavored to capture those publications and products that can best serve the professional interested in advancing his/her understanding of the Governance and Elections issues within the context of the whole of government approach and supplement what he/she can extract from this handbook.

2. Alphabetical listing of References – All Sources

a. African Union and New Partnership for Africa's Development. "African Post-Conflict Reconstruction Policy Framework." 2005.

b. Bolongaita, Emil. "Controlling Corruption in Post-conflict Countries." Occasional Paper #26. Kroc Institute: University of Notre Dame, January 2005.

c. Boucher, Alix; Durch, William J.; Midyette, Margaret; Rose, Sarah; and Terry, Jason. "Mapping and Fighting Corruption in War-Torn States." Stimson Center Report No. 61. Washington, DC: The Henry L. Stimson Center, March 2007.

d. Bryan, Shari. "Engaging Political Parties in Post-Conflict Parliaments." International Conference on Parliaments, Crisis Prevention and Recovery. Brussels, Belgium: April 19-20, 2006.

e. Building Civil Society in Post-Conflict Environments: From the Micro to the Macro. Occasional paper by the Woodrow Wilson International Center for Scholars. Washington, DC, November 2006. *http://www.wilsoncenter.org/topics/pubs/Ocpaper.pdf*.

f. Country Support Team (CST) Project Technical Team. "Strengthening the Capacity of Local Administration." 2008.

g. Covey, Jock, Michael J. Dziedzic, and Leonard R. Hawley (eds.). The Quest for Viable Peace: International Intervention and Strategies for Conflict Transformation. Washington DC: United States Institute of Peace Press, 2005.

h. DeGrasse, Beth Cole and Cristina Caan. Transitional Governance, From Bullets to Ballots, Washington, DC, US Institute of Peace, July 2006. *http://www.usip.org/pubs/specialreports/srs/srs2.html*.

i. Dobbins, James, Seth G. Jones, Keith Crane, and Beth Cole DeGrasse. The Beginner's Guide to Nation-Building. Santa Monica, CA: RAND Corporation, 2007.

j. European Commission. "Communication from the Commission to the Council, the European Parliament and the European Economic and Social Committee: Governance and Development." COM (2003) 615.

k. Geneva Centre for the Democratic control of Armed Forces (DCAF). "Parliamentary Committees on Defence and Security." DCAF Backgrounder, March 2006.

l. Geneva Centre for the Democratic control of Armed Forces (DCAF). "The Parliamentary Dimension of Defence Procurement: Requirements, Production, Cooperation and Acquisitions." DCAF Occasional Paper No. 5, March 2005.

m. Geneva Centre for the Democratic control of Armed Forces (DCAF). "Parliamentary Committees on Defence and Security."

n. Ghani, Ashraf and Clare Lockhart. Fixing Failed States: A Framework for Rebuilding a Fractured World. Oxford, United Kingdom: Oxford University Press, 2008.

o. Hart, Vivien. "Democratic Constitution Making." United States Institute of Peace, Special Report Number 107, July 2003. *http://www.usip.org/pubs/specialreports/sr107.pdf.*

p. Inbal, Aliza Belman and Lerner, Hanna. Governance in Post-conflict Societies: Rebuilding Fragile States. "Constitutional Design, Identify, and Legitimacy in Post-Conflict Reconstruction." New York: Routledge, 2007.

q. International Institute for Democracy and Electoral Assistance (IDEA). Assessing the Quality of Democracy: A Practical Guide. Stockholm: International IDEA, 2008. *http://www.idea.int/publications.*

r. International Institute for Democracy and Electoral Assistance (IDEA). Code of Conduct for Political Parties: Campaigning in Democratic Elections. 1999.

s. International Institute for Democracy and Electoral Assistance (IDEA). Effective Party Assistance: Stronger Parties for Better Democracy. IDEA, November 2007. *http://www.idea.int/publications.*

t. Joint Center for International Security Force Assistance (JCISFA). Commander's Handbook for Security Force Assistance. Fort Leavenworth, Kansas: JCISFA, July 2008.

u. Joint Publication 3-07.3. *Peace Operations*, 17 October 2007.

v. Joint Publication 3-57. *Civil Military Operations*, 8 July 2008.

w. Joint Publication 5-0. *Joint Operation Planning*, 26 December 2006.

x. Kaufmann, Daniel; Kraay, Aart; and Mastruzzi, Massimo. "Governance Matters IV." World Bank Policy Research No. 3630, May 2005.

y. Le Billon, P. "Overcoming Corruption in the Wake of Conflict." Transparency International (ed.), Global Corruption Report 2005. London: Pluto Press, 2005.

z. Liberia Field Team Report, 5-14 September 2007.

aa. Malan, Mark. Security Sector Reform in Liberia: Mixed Results from Humble Beginnings. Army War College Strategic Studies Institute, March 2008.

bb. Marenin, Otwin. "Restoring Policing Systems in Conflict Torn Nations: Process, Problems, Prospects." Geneva Centre for Democratic Control of Armed Forces (DCAF) Occasional Paper No. 7. Geneva: DCAF, June 2005.

cc. McFate, Sean. "Securing the Future: A Primer on Security Sector Reform in Conflict Countries." United States Institute of Peace Special Report 209. Washington, DC: United States Institute of Peace, September 2008.

dd. National Democratic Institute for International Affairs (NDI). A Guide to Political Party Development. Washington, DC: 2001. *http://www.accessdemocracy.org /library/1320 gdeppdev 102001.pdf#search='ivan%9620doherty.*

ee. National Democratic Institute for International Affairs (NDI). Assessing Women's Political Party Programs: Best Practices and Recommendations. Washington, DC: NDI, 2008.

ff. National Democratic Institute for International Affairs (NDI). Political Party Capacity Building Program Manual. Washington DC: *http://www.accessdemocracy.org /library/1719 na politicalpartiesmanual060104.pdf.*

gg. National Democratic Institute for International Affairs (NDI). Toward the Development of International Standards for Democratic Legislatures. NDI, January 2007.

hh. National Democratic Institute for International Affairs (NDI). Bosnia and Hercegovina (BiH): Strengthening Political Parties, Washington, DC: NDI, Spring 1996.

ii. Netherlands Institute of International Relations (Clingendael). "Lessons Learned in Political Party Assistance." The Hague: Seminar report, 4 November 2004. *http:// www.clingendael.nl/publications/2004/20041100 cru proc schoofs.pdf #search='political%party%20assistance.*

jj. Netherlands Institute for Multiparty Democracy (IMD). A Framework for Democratic Party Building: A Handbook. 2004. *http://wwe.nimd.org/upload/ publications/2004/imd institutional development handbook a4.pdf.*

kk. Organization for Economic Co-operation and Development (OECD). "Donor Approaches to Governance Assessments: Guiding Principles for Enhanced Impact, Usage and Harmonisation," OECD: March 2009.

ll. Organization for Economic Co-operation and Development. OECD DAC Handbook on Security System Reform: Supporting Security and Justice. OECD, 2007.

mm. Organization for Economic Co-operation and Development. Security System Reform and Governance. DAC Guidelines and Reference Series. OECD: 2005.

nn. Organization for Economic Co-operation and Development. "Fragile States: Policy Commitment and Principles for Good International Engagement in Fragile States and Situations." Development Co-operation Directorate and Development Assistance Committee. 2007.

oo. Panarelli, Liz. "The Role of the Ministerial Advisor in Security Sector Reform: Navigating Institutional Terrains." Washington DC: United States Institute of Peace, April 2009.

pp. Peacekeeping and Stability Operations Institute (PKSOI). "The Military Role in Rebuilding Governance in Stability Operations." PKSOI: January 2009.

qq. Perito, Robert M. "The Interior Ministry's Role in Security Sector Reform." United States Institute of Peace Special Report 223. Washington, DC: United States Institute of Peace, May 2009.

rr. RAND. Ungoverned Territories: Understanding and Reducing Terrorism Risks. RAND Corporation, 2007. *http://www.rand.org.*

ss. Samuels, Kirsti and Wyeth, Vanessa Hawkins. "State-building and Constitutional Design after Conflict." New York: International Peace Academy, 2006.

tt. The 9/11 Commission Report: Final Report of the National Commission on Terrorist Attacks Upon the United States. July 2004.

uu. The Challenges Project. "Meeting the Challenges of Peace Operations: Cooperation and Coordination." Elanders Gotab: Stockholm, 2005. *www.challengesproject.net.*

vv. Transparency International. Addressing Corruption and Building Integrity in Defense Establishments. TI Working Paper No. 2, 2007.

ww. Transparency International. The Corruption Fighters' Tool Kit. Berlin: Transparency International, 2002.

xx. Transparency International. TI Anti-Corruption Handbook: National Integrity System in Practice. *http://www.transparency.org/policy research/ach.*

yy. United Kingdom Department of International Development (DFID). "Security and Justice Sector Reform Programming in Africa." Evaluation Working Paper 23. London: DFID, April 2007.

zz. United Kingdom Department of International Development. "Stabilisation Tasks Matrix" (Version 1.0). 30 June 2008.

aaa. United Nations. "Tenth Report to the UN Security Council on IFOR Operations." 23 September 1996.

bbb. United Nations Development Programme (UNDP). A Handbook on Working with Political Parties, UNDP: New York, 2004(?).

ccc. United Nations Development Programme. A Users' Guide to Measuring Corruption. UNDP: 2008.

ddd. United Nations Development Programme. "Corruption and Good Governance." Discussion Paper 3. New York: UNDP, July 1997.

eee. United Nations Development Programme, UNDP's Engagement with Political Parties, July 2005.

fff. United Nations Development Programme and United States Agency for International Development (USAID). "First Steps in Post-Conflict State-Building: a UNDP-USAID Study. Draft Final Report." 2007.

ggg. United Nations Development Programme. "Security Sector Reform and Transitional Justice: A Crisis Post-Conflict Programmatic Approach." UNDP: March 2003.

hhh. United Nations Development Programme. "UNDP Anti-Corruption Practice Note: Mainstreaming Anti-Corruption in Development." UNDP, December 2008.

iii. United Nations Development Programme. Parliament, the Budget and Gender, UNDP Handbook for Parliamentarians, No. 6, 2004.

jjj. United Nations Development Programme. "Parliamentary Development: Practice Note." UNDP: April 2003.

kkk. United Nations Development Programme. "Parliaments, Crisis Prevention and Recovery: Guidelines for the International Community." UNDP: 2006.

lll. United Nations Development Programme. "UNDP Lessons Learned in Parliamentary Development." Institutional Development Group, Bureau for Development Policy, October 2002.

mmm. United Nations Development Programme. UNDP Strategy Note on Governance for Human Development. 2004.

nnn. US Agency for International Development. A Handbook on Fighting Corruption. Washington D.C: USAID, February 1999.

ooo. US Agency for International Development. "Anticorruption and Police Integrity." Washington, DC: USAID, May 2007.

ppp. US Agency for International Development (USAID). "Building Peace along Borders in East Africa." *http://www.usaid.gov/our work/cross cutting programs/conflict /success stories/east africa.*

qqq. US Agency for International Development. Civil Society Groups and Political Parties, Supporting Constructive Relationships. US Agency for International Development Occasional Paper, Washington, DC, March 2004. *http://www.usaid.gov/ our work//democracy and governance/publications/pdfs/pnacu631.pdf.*

rrr. US Agency for International Development. Conducting a DG Assessment: A Framework for Strategy Development. Washington, DC: November 2000.

sss. US Agency for International Development. Decentralization and Democratic Local Governance Programming Handbook. Washington, DC: May 2000. *http://www. usaid.gov/our work/democracy and governance/publications/pdfs/pnach300.pdf.*

ttt. US Agency for International Development. "Foreign Aid in the National Interest: Promoting Freedom, Security, and Opportunity." Washington, DC: USAID, 2002.

uuu. US Agency for International Development. "Fragile States Strategy." Washington, DC: USAID, January 2005.

vvv. US Agency for International Development. Handbook on Legislative Strengthening. Technical Publication Series. Center for Democracy and Governance, Bureau for Global Programs, Field Support, and Research. Washington, DC: USAID, 2000.

www. US Agency for International Development. Political Party Development Assistance, Washington, DC: USAID, April 1999.

xxx. US Agency for International Development. "Promoting Transparency and Accountability: USAID's Anti-corruption Experience." Washington, DC: USAID, January 2000.

yyy. US Agency for International Development, US Department of Defense and US Department of State. Security Sector Reform. Washington, DC: USAID, January 2009.

zzz. US Agency for International Development. USAID's Experience Strengthening Legislatures. Washington, DC: USAID, June 2001.

aaaa. US Agency for International Development. USAID's Experience in Decentralization and Democratic Local Governance. Washington, DC: September 2000. *http://www.usaid.gov/our work/democracy and governance/publications/pdfs/ pnach302.pdf.*

bbbb. US Agency for International Development. USAID Guidance for Democracy and Governance Programming in Post-Conflict (draft). Washington, DC: USAID, February 2009.

cccc. US Army Civil Affairs and Psychological Operations Command. Assessment of Governance Quality Indicators (AGQI) in Afghanistan: Initial Assessment in Three Afghan Cities Using a Standardized Assessment Tool and Potential Application of AGQI in Future Operations. 1 June 2005.

dddd. US Department of the Army. Civil Affairs Operations. Field Manual No. 3-05.40 (FM 41-10), 29 September 2006.

eeee. US Department of the Army. Counterinsurgency. Field Manual (FM) 3-24 (MCWP 3-33.5), December 2006. *www.us.army.mil.*

ffff. US Department of the Army. Security Force Assistance. Field Manual (FM) 3-07.1. May 2009.

gggg. US Department of the Army. Stability Operations (FM 3-07), October 2008.

hhhh. US Department of Defense. National Defense Strategy. Washington, DC, June 2008.

iiii. US Department of Defense. Office of the Deputy Assistant Secretary of Defense for Policy Planning (OUSD(P)). Ungoverned Areas and Threats from Safe Havens. 2008.

jjjj. US Department of Defense Directive 3000.05. Military Support for Stability, Security, Transition, and Reconstruction (SSTR) Operations. 28 November 2005.

kkkk. US Department of State, Office of the Coordinator for Reconstruction and stabilization (S/CRS). "Transition Elections And Political Processes In Reconstruction and stabilization Operations: Lessons Learned. A Guide for United States Government Planners." June 2007.

llll. US Department of State. "United States Government Draft Planning Framework for Reconstruction. Stabilization and Conflict Transformation. Practitioner's Guide" 2008.

mmmm. US Department of State. United States Participation in the United Nations, 2007. Report by the Secretary of State to the Congress, April 2009.

nnnn. US Department of State, Bureau of Political-Military Affairs. US Government Counterinsurgency Guide. Washington, DC: January 2009. *www.state.gov/t/pm/ppa/pmppt.*

oooo. US Department of State. Post-Conflict Reconstruction Essential Tasks. April 2005. *http://www.state.gov/documents/organization/53464.pdf.*

pppp. Ward, Celeste J. The Coalition Provisional Authority's Experience with Governance in Iraq: Lessons Identified. Washington DC, US Institute for Peace, Special Report No. 139, May 2005. *http://www.usip.org/pubs/specialreports/sr139.html.*

qqqq. Widner, Jennifer. "Constitution Writing and Conflict Resolution." Research Paper No. 2005/51. United Nations University-WIDER, August 2005.

rrrr. Willits-King, B. and Harvey, Paul. Managing the Risks of Corruption in Humanitarian Relief Operations. London: Overseas Development Institute, Humanitarian Policy Group, 2005.

ssss. World Bank. Helping Countries Combat Corruption. June 2000.

tttt. Zeeuw, Jeroen de (ed.). From Soldiers to Politicians: Transforming Rebel Movements after Civil War. Boulder, Colorado: Lynne Rienner Publishers, 2008.

3. Web Sites for Key Stakeholders, Donors, and Implementing Partners

a. US Government Agencies

(1) Department of State – http://www.state.gov

(a) Regional Bureaus:

1. Africa (AF)

2. East Asian and Pacific Affairs (EAP)

3. European and Eurasian Affairs (EUR)

4. Near Eastern Affairs (NEA)

5. South and Central Asian Affairs (SCA)

6. Western Hemispheric Affairs (WHA)

(b) Bureau of Democracy Human Rights and Labor

(c) Bureau of International Narcotics and Law Enforcement Affairs

(d) Bureau of Political-Military Affairs

(e) Bureau of Population, Refugees and Migration

(f) Office of the Coordinator for Reconstruction and stabilization

(2) US Agency for International Development (USAID) – http://www.usaid.gov

(a) Office of Democracy and Governance

(b) Office of Military Affairs

(c) Office of Transition Initiatives

b. **Major Foreign Government Development Agencies**

(1) Australia: Agency for International Development (AUSAID) – http://www.ausaid.gov.au

(2) Canada: Canadian International Development Agency (CIDA) – http://www.acdi-cida.gc.ca

(3) France: French Development Agency/Agence Francaise de Developpment (AFD) – http://www.afd.fr/jahia/lang/en/home

(4) Germany: German Agency for Technical Cooperation/Deutsche Gesellschaft für Technische Zusammenarbeit (GTZ) GmbH – http://www.gtz.de/en/index/htm

(5) Japan: Japan International Cooperation Agency (JICA) – http://www.jica.go.jp/english/

(6) New Zealand: International Aid and Development Agency (NZAID) – http://www.nzaid.govt.nz

(7) Norway: Norwegian Agency for Development Cooperation (Norad) – http://norad.no/en

(8) Sweden: Swedish International Development Cooperation Agency (SIDA) – http://www.sida.se/?language=en_us

(9) United Kingdom: Department for International Development (DFID) – http://www.dfid.gov.uk

(10) UK Government's Stabilisation Unit – http://www.stabilisationunit.gov.uk

c. **International Organizations**

(1) International Institute for Democracy and Electoral Assistance – http://www.idea.int

(2) Organization for Economic Coordination and Development (OECD) – http://www.oecd.org

(3) Organization for Security and Cooperation in Europe (OSCE) – http://www.osce.org

(4) Office for Democratic Institutions and Human Rights (ODIHR) – http://www.osce.org/odihr

(5) UN Peacekeeping – http://www.un.org/Depts/dpko/dpko/dpko.shtml

(6) UN Development Program – http://www.undp.org

(7) United Nations Educational, Scientific and Cultural Organization – http://www.unesco.org

d. Nongovernmental Organizations

(1) International Committee of the Red Cross – http://icrc.org

(2) American Center for International Labor Solidarity – http://www.solidaritycenter.org

(3) Center for International Private Enterprise (CIPE) – http://www.cipe.org

(4) Management Systems International (MSI) – http://www.msi-inc.com

(5) National Democratic Institute – http://www.ndi.org

(6) National Endowment for Democracy – http://www.ned.org

(7) International Foundation for Electoral Systems (IFES) – http://www.ifes.org

(8) International Republican Institute – http://www.iri.org

(9) RTI International – http://www.rti.org

(10) US Institute of Peace – http://www.usip.org

APPENDIX E
ENDNOTES

[1] The term "post-conflict" is used in this handbook for simplicity to describe both the environment immediately following combat operations ("first response") and to describe the early stages of stabilization and reconstruction operations.

[2] FM 3-07, *Stability Operations*, p. 5-2. Military government or transitional military authority is a temporary military government exercising the functions of civil administration in the absence of a legitimate civil authority.

[3] See: Should Military Governance Guidance Return to its Roots? A Doctrinal Comparison Between FM 27-5 (1943) and FM 3-05.40 (2006), by Colonel Hugh Vanroosen, United States Army. (www.csl.army.mil/.../S02 09 Vanroosen ShouldMilitary GovernanceGuidanceReturnToItsRoots.pdf)

[4] Nine major interventions have occurred during the Post-Cold War period: Iraq (twice), Somalia, Bosnia, Haiti, Rwanda, Kosovo, East Timor and Afghanistan. Panama and Granada occurred prior to this period.

[5] This has happened frequently in the past. Liberia, Sierra Leone, and Cambodia are recent examples.

[6] Secretary of Defense Robert M. Gates, speech at the National Defense University, September 29, 2008.

[7] FM 3-07, *Stability Operations*, October 2008.

[8] FM 3-24/MCWP 3-33.5, pp. 5-5.

[9] FM 3-07, *Stability Operations*, p. 1-1.

[10] FM 3-07, *Stability Operations*, provides a useful summary of the American experience with Stability Operations, of which governance is a key component. See pp. 1-1, 1-2.

[11] Tenth report to the UN Security Council on IFOR Operations, 23 September 1996.

[12] UNDP Strategy Note on Governance for Human Development, 2004.

[13] Daniel Kaufmann, Aart Kraay, and Massimo Mastruzzi, "Governance Matters IV," World Bank Policy Research No. 3630 (May 2005).

[14] European Commission, "Communication from the Commission to the Council, the European Parliament and the European Economic and Social Committee: Governance and Development," COM (2003) 615.

[15] "USAID Primer: What We Do and How We Do It." United States Agency for International Development, 2006.

16 Draft "USAID Guidance For Democracy And Governance Programming In Post-Conflict Countries," Office of Democracy and Governance, Bureau of Democracy, Conflict, and Humanitarian Assistance, US Agency for International Development, May 2009, p. 5.

17 FM 3-07, *Stability Operations*, pp 1.17-1.18.

18 USAID, "Foreign Aid in the National Interest: Promoting Freedom, Security, and Opportunity," (Washington, DC: USAID, 2002).

19 USAID, "Fragile States Strategy," (January 2005) p. 3.

20 JP 1-02, *Department of Defense Dictionary of Military and Associated Terms*; JP 3-0, *Joint Operations*.

21 Draft Principles for Stabilization, Reconstruction, and Social Transformation. Office of the Coordinator for Reconstruction and Stabilization (S/CRS), US Department of State, August 2006.

22 JP 5-0, *Joint Operation Planning*, Chapter IV, "Operational Art and Design."

23 United States Participation in the United Nations, 2007, pp. 63-64. Report by the Secretary of State to the Congress, April 2009.

24 JP 3-57, *Civil Military Operations*, II-34.

25 USAID's implementing partners (IP) are also likely to be in-country or to soon arrive. Typical governance and political development IPs are NDI, IRI, TAF, RTI, IFES (see Appendix X for full names).

26 FM 3-07, *Stability Operations*, pp. 1-18. FM 3-07 defines whole of government as "an approach that integrates the collaborative efforts of the departments and agencies of the United States Government to achieve unity of effort toward a shared goal."

27 FM 3-07, *Stability Operations*.

28 FM 3-07, *Stability Operations*, pp 1.3 -1.5.

29 JP 1-02, *Department of Defense Dictionary of Military and Associated Terms*, p. 575.

30 FM 3-07, *Stability Operations*, pp. 1-3.

31 JP 3-57, p. I-15; FM 3-5.40, *Civil Affairs Operations*, p. 2-4.

32 USAID Guidance for Democracy and Governance in Post-Conflict Countries, (draft), February 2009, p. 7.

33 JP 5-0, *Joint Operational Planning*, Chapter IV.

[34] For further elaboration, see United States Department of the Army, FM 3-07, *Stability Operations*, October 2008, pp. 1-10 to 1-1-16.

[35] 2009 Congressional Budget Justification (CBJ) for Foreign Operations, http://www.usaid.gov/policy/budget/cbj2009/101468.pdf.

[36] FM 3-07, *Stability Operations*, (Glossary-2): "1. A continuous process that measures the overall effectiveness of employing joint force capabilities during military operations. 2. Determination of the progress toward accomplishing a task, creating an effect, or achieving an objective. 3. Analysis of the security, effectiveness, and potential of an existing or planned intelligence activity. 4. Judgment of the motives, qualifications, and characteristics of present or prospective employees or "agents. (JP 3-0) (Army) The continuous monitoring and evaluation of the current situation and progress of an operation. (FM 3-0)."

[37] USAID's Office of Democracy and Governance is revising the DG Assessment Framework in 2009. The following is based on the outline of the revisions that are in the process of being finalized.

[38] FM 3-07, *Stability Operations*, includes a detailed overview of ICAF in Appendix D, pp. D-1 to D-13. However, FM 3-07 notes that the information on ICAF is for information only and that the military uses doctrinal assessment tools for understanding, planning and execution. ICAF may "inform, but not replace those doctrinal tools."

[39] USAID, Conducting A DG Assessment: A Framework for Strategy Development, 2000.

[40] JP 5-0, see especially Chapter III, paragraph 15, "Course of Action Comparison," pp. III-32- III-34.

[41] Democracy and Governance Assessment of Tanzania: Transitions from a Single-Part State, Burlington, Vermont: ARD, Inc., November 2003.

[42] OECD "Donor Approaches to Governance Assessments: Guiding Principles for Enhanced Impact, Usage and Harmonisation," March 2009, p. 2.

[43] Ibid, p. 1.

[44] Joint CSIS/AUSA Post-Conflict Reconstruction (PCR) Task Framework" from Winning the Peace: An American Strategy for Post-Conflict Reconstruction, edited by Robert C. Orr. CSIS Press, 2004.

[45] Post-conflict military support to Elections and Media Development are discussed in Chapters 4 and 5, respectively. These subjects have separate chapters because the military role is substantial in a post-conflict and transitional environment, although often not acknowledged by DOD or commanders.

[46] Bryan, Shari, "Engaging Political Parties in Post-Conflict Parliaments," International Conference on Parliaments, Crisis Prevention and Recovery, Brussels, Belgium, April 19-20, 2006.

[47] Celeste J. Ward; The Coalition Provisional Authority's Experience with Governance in Iraq: Lessons Identified, Special Report No. 139, US Institute for Peace, Washington, DC, May 2005.

[48] JP 5-0, p. IV-2.

[49] Hard Lessons: The Iraq Reconstruction Experience. Report of the Special Inspector General for Iraq Reconstruction, US Government Printing Office, Washington, D.C., February 2009.

[50] DeGrasse, Beth Cole and Cristina Caan. Transitional Governance, From Bullets to Ballots, Washington, DC, US Institute of Peace, July 2006. http://www.usip.org/pubs/specialreports/srs/srs2.html.

[51] Decentralization and Democratic Local Governance Programming Handbook, p. 40, US Agency for International Development, Washington, DC, May 2000, http://www.usaid.gov/our work/democracy and governance/publications/pdfs/pnach300.pdf.

[52] James A. Gavrillis, "The Mayor of Ar Rutbah", Foreign Policy, November/December 2005.

[53] Ward, Celeste J., The Coalition Provisional Authority's Experience with Governance in Iraq: Lessons Identified, Special Report No. 139, US Institute for Peace, Washington, DC, May 2005. http://www.usip.org/pubs/specialreports/sr139.html.

[54] USAID's Experience in Decentralization and Democratic Local Governance, p. 7. US Agency for International Development, Center for Democracy and Development, Washington, DC, September 2000. (http://www.usaid.gov/our work/democracy and governance/publications/pdfs/pnach302.pdf)

[55] Geneva Centre for the Democratic control of Armed Forces (DCAF), "Parliamentary Committees on Defence and Security," DCAF Backgrounder, March 2006, p. 1.

[56] For further details, see DCAF, "The Parliamentary Dimension of Defence Procurement: Requirements, Production, Cooperation and Acquisitions," DCAF Occasional Paper No. 5, March 2005.

[57] DCAF, "Parliamentary Committees on Defence and Security, p. 3.

[58] United Nations Development Programme (UNDP), "Parliamentary Development: Practice Note, April 2003.

[59] United State Agency for International Development (USAID), "USAID's Experience Strengthening Legislatures," Washington, D.C.: USAID, June 2001, pp. 20-21.

[60] UNDP, "Parliaments, Crisis Prevention and Recovery: Guidelines for the International Community, "UNDP, 2006, pp. 7-9.

[61] United States Agency for International Development, Political Party Development Assistance, Washington, D.C.: USAID, April 1999, p. 12. (www.usaid.gov/our work/ democracy and governance/publications)

[62] United Nations Development Programme, UNDP's Engagement with Political Parties, July 2005.

[63] For a more detailed review of international donors, see International Institute for Democracy and Electoral Assistance (IDEA), Effective Party Assistance: Stronger Parties for Better Democracy, IDEA, November 2007, pp. 11-14. (http://www.idea.int/ publications)

[64] USAID, Political Party Development Assistance, pp. 24-25.

[65] National Democratic Institute for International Affairs (NDI), Bosnia and Hercegovina (BiH): Strengthening Political Parties, Washington, D.C.: NDI, Spring 1996, pp. 20.

[66] Ibid. p. 23.

[67] Ibid, p. 2-5.

[68] NDI, Assessing Women's Political Party Programs: Best Practices and Recommendations 2008, p. 3 and p. 46.

[69] Ibid. pp. 59-60, p. 62.

[70] Department for International Development (DFID), "Stabilisation Tasks Matrix" (Version 1.0), 30 June 2008, p. 25.

[71] United Nations Development Programme (UNDP), A Handbook on Working with Political Parties, UNDP: New York, 2004(?), pp. 41-42.

[72] This handbook uses the term "political reconciliation" to mean nonviolent, political engagement with or between conflicting parties with the intent of rendering possible and then establishing a peaceful relationship between them, a definition adopted from Michael Semple, Reconciliation in Afghanistan, Washington: United States Institute of Peace, 2009, p. 1.

[73] Willits-King, B. and Paul Harvey, Managing the Risks of Corruption in Humanitarian Relief Operations. London: Overseas Development Institute, Humanitarian Policy Group, 2005, p. 1. (http://www.odi.org.uk/resources/download/1333.pdf)

[74] Special Inspector General for Iraq Reconstruction (SIGIR), Hard Lessons: The Iraq Reconstruction Experience. Washington, DC: US Government Printing Office, 2009, page

211. (http://www.sigir.mil/hardlessons/Default.aspx)

[75] Mohmoud Othman, independent member of Parliament, Iraq. Quoted in The Washington Post, May 10, 2009.

[76] Office of the Special Inspector General for Iraq Reconstruction (SIGIR), US Anticorruption Efforts in Iraq: Progress Made in Implementing Revised Management Plan, 2008. (http://www.sigir.mil/reports/pdf/audits/08-016.pdf)

[77] Transparency International, Addressing Corruption and Building Integrity in Defence Establishments, TI Working Paper No. 2, 2007, p. 3. (http://www.transparency.org/publications/publications/working papers/working paper no 2 defence)

[78] Office of the Special Inspector General for Iraq Reconstruction (SIGIR), Hard Lessons: The Iraq Reconstruction Experience. Washington, DC: US Government Printing Office, 2009, pages 206-16. (http://www.sigir.mil/hardlessons/Default.aspx)

[79] See DODD 5132.03, *DoD Policy and Responsibilities Relating to Security Cooperation*, (Oct. 24, 2008): security assistance. A group of programs authorized by Title 22, United States Code, as amended, or other related statutes by which the United States provides defense articles, military training, and other defense-related services by grant, loan, credit, cash sales, or lease, in furtherance of national policies and objectives. The Department of Defense does not administer all security assistance programs. Those security assistance programs that are administered by the Department are a subset of security cooperation.

[80] US Department of the Army, FM 3-07.1, *Security Force Assistance*, p. 1-1; and Joint Center for International Security Force Assistance (JCISFA), *Commander's Handbook for Security Force Assistance*, p. 1-7.

[81] See DODD, 5132.3, *DoD Policy and Responsibilities Relating to Security Cooperation* (October 24, 2008); and JP 3-07.1, *Foreign Internal Defense*, pp. V-8 to V-12, concerning security assistance (SA).

[82] JP 3-07.1, *Foreign Internal Defense*, states, "SA is the provision of defense articles, military training, and other defense-related services by grant, loan, credit, or cash sales in furtherance of US national policies and objectives."

[83] FM 3-07, *Stability Operations*, p. 2-3.

[84] Ibid.

[85] SOF's previously more limited SFA role is discussed in joint doctrine as Foreign Internal Defense (FID) and HN Military Assistance. See JP 3-05, *Joint Special Operations*, p. II-7.

[86] Ibid., p. 9 (Glossary).

[87] FM 3-07.1, p. 1-1; JCISFA, *Commander's Handbook for Security Force Assistance*, p. 1.

[88] US Agency for International Development, US Department of Defense, and US Department of State, Security Sector Reform, February 2009, p 3.

[89] Ibid, p 3.

[90] Ibid, p 4.

[91] McFate, Sean, "Securing the Future: A Primer on Security Sector Reform in Conflict Countries," United States Institute of Peace Special Report 209, September 2008, pp. 15-16.

[92] Also see Malan, Mark, Security Sector Reform in Liberia: Mixed Results from Humble Beginnings, Army War College Strategic Studies Institute, March 2008, p. v.

[93] Ibid. p. 2-2; JCISFA, *Commander's Handbook for Security Force Assistance*, p. 5.

[94] JCISFA, *Commander's Handbook for Security Force Assistance*, p. 6.

[95] Support of the UN Secretary-General, Securing Peace and Development: The Role of the United Nations in Supporting Security Sector Reform, 23 January 2008, p 5-7.

[96] JP 5-0, pp. IV-4 to IV-32.

[97] Department of International Development (DFID), "Security and Justice Sector Reform Programming in Africa." Evaluation Working Paper 23. London: DFID, April 2007, p. 23.

[98] Ibid. p. 32.

[99] Perito, Robert M., "The Interior Ministry's Role in Security Sector Reform," United States Institute of Peace Special Report 223, Washington, D.C.: United States Institute of Peace, May 2009, p. 3.

[100] Panerelli, Liz, "The Role of the Ministerial Advisor in Security Sector Reform: Navigating Institutional Terrains," Washington D.C.: United States Institute of Peace, April 2009, p. 3.

[101] Organisation for Economic Co-operation and Development (OECD), OECD DAC Handbook on Security System Reform: Supporting Security and Justice. OECD, 2007, p. 22.

[102] Office of the Deputy Assistant Secretary of Defense for Policy Planning (OUSD(P)), Ungoverned Areas and Threats from Safe Havens, 2008.

[103] The 9/11 Commission Report, July 2004, p. 366.

[104] Department of Defense, *National Defense Strategy*, June 2008, p. 3.

[105] Ungoverned Territories: Understanding and Reducing Terrorism Risks, www.rand.org/pubs/monographs/2007/RAND MG561.pdf, RAND Corporation, 2007, p. xv.

[106] Ungoverned Areas and Threats from Safe Havens, www.cissm.umd.edu/papers/files/ugash report final.pdf, p. 6.

[107] United States Agency for International Development (USAID), "Building Peace along Borders in East Africa," http://www.usaid.gov/our work/cross-cutting programs/conflict/success stories/east-Africa.

[108] *National Defense Strategy*, p. 3.

[109] Ibid, p. 23.

[110] FM 3-24 is not authoritative for joint forces. It is a Service publication. JP 3-24 will be authoritative joint doctrine.

[111] *US Government Counterinsurgency Guide*, pp. 6, 12. The definitions used in FM 3-24 are slightly different, citing joint doctrine (JP 1-02) to define insurgency as an organized movement aimed at the overthrow of a constituted government through the use of subversion and armed conflict. FM 3-24 defines counterinsurgency as "military, paramilitary, political, economic, psychological and civic actions taken by a government to defeat insurgency."

[112] *US Government Counterinsurgency Guide*, pp. 14-15.

[113] Ibid, p. 3.

[114] FM 3-24, *Counterinsurgency*, p. 5-3.

[115] Ibid, p. 24.

[116] *US Government Counterinsurgency Guide*, p. 4.

[117] United Nations, Peacekeeping Best Practices Section, The 2004 Presidential Election in Afghanistan: Lessons Learned (New York: 2005), 5.

[118] Transition Elections and Political Processes in Reconstruction and Stabilization Operations: Lessons Learned, Office of the Coordinator for Stabilization and Reconstruction (S/CRS), US Department of State. Washington, DC November 2007.

[119] Article 25, International Covenant on Civil and Political Rights, entered into force March 23, 1976.

[120] Barrick, Major Timothy E., Military Support to Post-Conflict Elections: Applying the lessons of the 2004 Afghan Presidential Election. Paper submitted to the faculty of the

Naval War College, Newport, RI, February 13, 2006.

[121] United Nations, *Handbook on UN Multidimensional Peacekeeping Operations*, Nov 2003.

[122] Himelfarb, Sheldon, "Media and peacebuilding: the new army stability doctrine and media sector development, Media, War & Conflict, SAGE Pub, Los Angeles, 2009 Principles herein listed are from the article but have been modified in some places to reflect level of military participation, i.e., GCC vice Army.

[123] "Liberated and Occupied Iraq: New Beginnings and Challenges for Press Freedom," special report from Freedom House, Washington DC, August 2004, p. 5.

[124] Barry Bearak, "A Massive Phenomenon in Afghanistan: Television," The New York Times, July 31, 2007.

[125] *DOD Financial Management Regulation*, Volume 12, Chapter 27, Annex A, January 2009.

[126] FM 3-07, *Stability Operations*.

[127] Himelfarb, Sheldon, "Media and Peacebuilding: The New Army Stability Doctrine and Media Sector Development," Media, War & Conflict, SAGE Pub, Los Angeles, 2009.

[128] Drawn from International IDEA, Assessing the Quality of democracy: A Practical Guide, Stockholm: International IDEA, 2008.

Intentionally Blank

GLOSSARY
PART I—ABBREVIATIONS AND ACRONYMS

ADF	America's Development Foundation
AMEMB	American Embassy
CA	civil affairs
CAII	Creative Associates International Inc
CCDR	Combatant Commander
CERP	Commander's Emergency Response Program
CIDA	Canadian International Development Agency
CMO	Civil Military Operations
CMOC	Civil Military Operations Center
CORDS	Civil Operation and Revolutionary Development Support
COIN	counter-insurgency operations
CPA	Coalition Provisional Authority
CRSG	Country Reconstruction & Stabilization Group
CSP	Community Stabilization Programs
DCHA/CMM	USAID Office of Conflict Management and Mitigation
DDR	disarmament, demobilization, and reintegration
DFI	Development Fund for Iraq
DFID	United Kingdom Department for International Development
DG	US Agency for International Development Office of Democracy and Governance programs
DI	Democracy International
DOD	Department of Defense
DODD	Department of Defense Directive
DOS	Department of State
DRL	DOS Bureau of Democracy, Human Rights and Labor
ETM	DOS Coordinator for Reconstruction and Stabilization essential task matrix
EU	European Union
FID	foreign internal defense
FM	Field Manual
FY	fiscal year
GAP	UN Government Assessment Portal
GCC	geographic combatant commander
HA	humanitarian assistance
HN	Host Nation
HRDF	DOS Human Rights Democracy Fund

IBRD	International Bank for Reconstruction and Development
IDA	International Development Association
ICAF	Interagency Conflict Assessment Framework
IDP	internally displaced person (or population)
IGO	intergovernmental organization
IFES	International Foundation for Electoral Systems
IFOR	Implementation Force (Bosnia)
IMS	interagency management system
INL	DOS Bureau of International Narcotics and Law Enforcement
IO	international organization
IP	USAID implementation partners
IPDC	International Program for the Development of Communication
IREX	International Research and Exchanges Board
IRI	International Republican Institute
ISAF	International Security Assistance Force (Afghanistan)
ITU	International Telecommunications Union
IWPR	Institute for War and Peace Reporting
JFC	joint force commander
JTF	joint task force
JP	joint publication
LOE	line of effort
LOO	line of operations
MCA	military civic action
MME	main mission element
MPICE	measuring progress in conflict environments
MSI	Management Systems International
NATO	North Atlantic Treaty Organization
NGO	nongovernmental organization
NDI	National Democratic Institute for International Affairs
NSPD	National Security Presidential Directive
NGO	nongovernmental organization
OAS	Organization of American States
OECD	Organization for Economic Cooperation and Development
OFDA	Office of US Foreign Disaster Assistance
OMA	USAID Office of Military Affairs
OSCE	Organisation for Security and Cooperation in Europe
OTI	USAID Office of Transition Initiatives

PA	public affairs
PSYOP	psychological operations
RSF	Reporters sans frontières
RTI	Research Triangle Institute
SA	security assistance
S/CRS	State Department of the Coordinator for Reconstruction and Stabilization
SFA	Security Force Assistance
SIDA	Sweden's International Development Cooperation Agency
SRSG	United Nations Special Representative of the Secretary General
SSR	Security Sector Reform
TOA	transfer of authorities; transition of authority
TAF	The Asia Foundation
UA	unified action
UGA/SH	ungoverned area/safe havens
UN	United Nations
UNDP	United Nations Development Programme
UN/DPA	UN Department of Political Affairs
UN/DPKO	UN Department of Peacekeeping Operations
UN/DESA	UN Department of Economic and Social Affairs
UNEAD	UN Electoral Assistance Division
UNESCO	UN United Nations Educational, Scientific and Cultural Organization
UNHCR	United Nations Office of the High Commissioner for Refugees
UNTAET	UN Transitional Administration in Timor-Leste
UNOPS	UN Office for Project Services
USAID	United States Agency for International Development
USIP	US Institute for Peace
USJFCOM	United States Joint Forces Command
USCAPOC	United States Army Civil Affairs and Psychological Operations Command
USG	United States Government
WB	World Bank
WFD	Westminster Foundation for Democracy

Intentionally Blank

PART II—TERMS AND DEFINITIONS

assessment. The continuous monitoring and evaluation of the progress of an operation.

development (also international development). Foreign assistance to improve HN institutions such as governance, rule of law, human rights, and gender equality. Development is related to foreign assistance, and is distinct from the concepts of security assistance, disaster relief and humanitarian assistance. Development also implies a longer-term perspective and planning cycle.

democratization. The process of political change that moves the political system of any society towards a system of government that ensures peaceful competitive political participation in an environment that guarantees political and civil liberties. It is sometimes paired with "governance" as in "democracy and governance" or with "political development."

evaluation. The process of determining the progress toward accomplishing a task or achieving an objective.

failed or fragile state. A country suffering from institutional weaknesses serious enough to threaten the stability of the central government.

golden hour. Derived from the medical context of the immediate post-triage period, the golden hour is that period of time (of whatever duration) immediately following an intervention or conclusion of a crisis, when authority structures, customary relationships, and familiar procedures have come unmoored from civil society. Decisions made during this period will have far-reaching impact by becoming the new standard around which a fractured society will coalesce as they reorganize themselves for the future. Popular tolerance of outside entities is usually higher during this period. In the context of a post-conflict environment, it can last up to a year following the initial intervention.

intergovernmental organization. An organization created by a formal agreement (e.g., a treaty) between two or more governments. It may be established on a global, regional, or functional basis for wide-ranging or narrowly defined purposes. Formed to protect and promote national interests shared by member states. Examples include the United Nations, North Atlantic Treaty Organization, and the African Union. Also called **IGO**. (JP 1-02, SOURCE: JP 3-08)

nation assistance. Civil or military assistance (other than foreign humanitarian assistance) provided to a country by US forces within that country's territory during peacetime, crises, or emergencies, or war, based on agreements mutually concluded between the United States and that country. Nation assistance operations support a host country by promoting sustainable development and growth of responsive institutions. The goal is to promote long-term regional stability. Nation assistance programs often include, but are not limited to, security assistance (SA), foreign internal defense (FID), and Title 10 United States Code (10 USC) programs, such as military civic action (MCA), and activities performed on a reimbursable basis by federal agencies or intergovernmental organizations. All nation assistance activities are normally coordinated with the US Ambassador through the Embassy Country Team

post conflict. The period following conflict and the cessation of active combat.

nongovernmental organization. A private, self-governing, not-for-profit organization dedicated to alleviating human suffering; and/or promoting education, health care, economic development, environmental protection, human rights, and conflict resolution; and/or encouraging the establishment of democratic institutions and civil society. Also called **NGO**. (JP 1-02, SOURCE: JP 3-08)

reconstruction. The process of rebuilding degraded, damaged or destroyed political, socioeconomic, and physical infrastructure of a country or territory to create the foundation for long-term development.

stabilization. The process by which underlying tensions that might lead to resurgence in violence and a breakdown in law and order are managed and reduced, while efforts are made to support preconditions for successful long-term development.

state building or reconstruction. The effort to build or rebuild the institutions of a weak, post-conflict, or failing state. State building may be undertaken following a military intervention or peacekeeping operation, or by regional or HN institutions. In a post-conflict environment, state building ideally involves external and internal actors constructively engaged in a process that results in political understandings on the form of government, prioritization and initiation of work to restore core government functions, and the provision of government services in response to public expectations. In this context, the term state building is preferable to "nation building," since it focuses on institutions rather than identity (a nation).

transparency. Openness and clarity in government, accounting and financing, or other decisions.

unified action. The synchronization, coordination, and/or integration of the activities of governmental and nongovernmental entities with military operations to achieve unity of effort. (JP 1-02, SOURCE: JP 1)

unity of effort. Coordination and cooperation toward common objectives, even if the participants are not necessarily part of the same command or organization - the product of successful unified action. (JP 1-02, SOURCE: JP 1)